IMAGES
of England

SOUTHBOROUGH
AND HIGH BROOMS

SOUTHBOROUGH
LOCAL BOARD

£1 REWARD.

WILFUL AND WANTON
DAMAGE.

WHEREAS, on Sunday night, the 10th August instant, and upon several previous nights, wilful and wanton damage has been committed by some evil disposed persons or person, in taking up and damaging the Seats on the Common, breaking down and damaging Stiles, Fences, and Tree Guards in various places in Southborough, and also committing many other acts of malicious damage to property.

NOTICE IS HEREBY GIVEN,

that the above Reward will be paid to any person giving such information to the undersigned as will lead to the conviction of the offenders.

Dated this 11th day of August, 1890.

PHILIP HANMER,

Clerk to Local Board.

Local Board Offices, Southborough.

J. H. CANE, Printer, 92, London Road, Southborough.

IMAGES
of England

SOUTHBOROUGH
AND HIGH BROOMS

Compiled by
Chris McCooey

TEMPUS

First published 1998, reprinted 1999
Copyright © Chris McCooey, 1998

Tempus Publishing Limited
The Mill, Brimscombe Port,
Stroud, Gloucestershire, GL5 2QG

ISBN 0 7524 1153 5

Typesetting and origination by
Tempus Publishing Limited
Printed in Great Britain by
Midway Clark Printing, Wiltshire

Two pre-Second World War postcards extolling Southborough's outdoor sporting and healthy attractions.

Contents

Oak & Grove Cottages, Southborough.

Cat's Castle on the Common just north of St Peter's church has also been called the Terrace and Grey Lodge and Oak and Grove Cottages. It may have got its current name from the Carter family who operated a sawmill pit on the site in the late eighteenth century. In earlier times there was a tradition that if a man could erect a dwelling on common land between sunset and sunrise he could live in it. Robert Carter certainly erected a woodshed on the site and carried on his wood cutting business there. The shed was extended over the years and became his home as well. During the nineteenth century the Carter family was often in dispute with the local authorities over whether they had title to the land and so the name may be an ironic contraction of Carter's Castle. Another possible explanation was provided by Gladys Sayer, a resident of Southborough, who wrote to *Southborough Spotlight* in February 1972 and said that her mother used to be a maid sometime in the 1880s to two old ladies called Walthew who lived in the cottage. The ladies kept chickens and they had the run of the Common and they also had many cats which were expected to keep down the rats that pinched the eggs. One of the maid's duties was to round up the chickens and shut them in for the night because of the foxes. The maid was paid 2s a week plus bed and board and her bedroom was approached by ladder through a trap door.

Introduction

This book has my name on the front cover but in fact it is a joint effort between myself and two others.

I never knew Doug Bennett personally but over many years he faithfully collected and collated all manner of material relating to Southborough and High Brooms. Doug fully intended to write the definitive history of the two towns and in preparation for that he regularly contributed interesting features to the Southborough Society's newsletters and gave talks to friends and societies who were interested in local history. Unfortunately Doug died before a book could appear; his widow, most generously, gave all his papers and photographs relating to Southborough and High Brooms to the Southborough Society and to Southborough Library. Thanks to Doug's hard work and assiduous sleuthing locally, my job has been a comparatively easy one of reading through his 130 folders, and selecting and editing the material to write the captions.

The other person whose name should be with Doug's and mine on the front cover is Maxwell Macfarlane. Maxwell is the oldest twelve-year-old I know – his enthusiasm and energy are infectious. I am very grateful to Maxwell for his generosity in making all of his knowledge and material (postcards, monographs, photographs, etc.) on local history available to me. It has been great fun working with Bald Eagle on this project.

Many of the photographs used have been obtained by Maxwell after talking to local residents; his notes, names put to faces in old photographs, and the reminiscences of local people are an important contribution to our local history. Maxwell would like to thank all the people who have helped him in his research and, in particular, the following: Mr and Mrs Fred Waghorn, Mrs Win Jenner, Mrs J.E. Cosham, Miss Queenie Latter, Mrs Ethel Cocks, Mr Tommy Culmer, Mr Fred Ongley, Mrs E. Goodland, Mr and Mrs Ron Bryant, Mrs May Steadman, Mrs Emily Dadswell, Miss Helen Clarke, Mr Alec Brown, Mr Bob Pring, Mr Sidney Whitlock, Mrs Norah Divall, Mrs Queen Acott, Mr Les Jeffery, Mr George Corbett and Mr George Paine of the baking family, who, sadly, died this year.

Many other people have helped – either by lending material or offering information. I would like to thank them personally. First, thank you to Martin Oxley, editor of the *Kent and Sussex Courier*, who published an open letter of mine soliciting old photographs – it produced a number of good leads. Then, in no particular order, they are: Peter Barrett for the history of Southborough Fire Brigade; Fred Howe for help on Broomhill and the Salomons; Mary Moore at Age Concern; Graham Pentecost – after forty-nine years working for the Town Council, most of which as the Clerk, this makes him positively encyclopaedic on Southborough and High Brooms since the Second World War; Frank Chapman, a.k.a. Warwick, of the *Courier*; Ann Kennedy on the Scouts; Eileen Rabbitt, erstwhile landlady of the Beehive now, sadly for the drinking classes, closed; Chris Waterman (*née* Bryant); Betty Hayden; Fred Scales; John Kennedy; Alan Waters; Mrs Harrison of Powdermill Lane; Roger Edwards; Mrs Ballard of Birchett's Lodge; Patricia Moon, the head librarian, and all of the staff of Southborough Library; Paul Russell, the new Town Clerk and morning Maureen and afternoon Mary in the office of the Council; Colin Young of Southborough Cricket Club; Mrs Jean Phillips-Martinsson; Keith Hetherington on the pubs of Southborough and history of High Brooms Brick and Tile Company; Malcolm Mills; Kathleen Strange for proof reading; Albert Dungate; Margaret Brooks; Bill Gowin for Buffalo information; Tuncer Mumcuoglu, proprietor of the Weavers; Mrs Everest of High Brooms; Vic Bethell of David Salomons; Margaret Clifton; Jock Ross; John Hudgell for cricket ball making information; Frank Stevens for research on the *Hythe* disaster; Mrs Jill Wickens (*née* Groves) for identifying workers at Paine Smith, the bakers; and, finally, as they say on *News at Ten*, the girl in Minute Man in St John's Road where I did my photocopying. It is to be recommended – she has a lovely smile.

By the nature of the exercise – trying to piece together little snippets of history, make sense of sometimes conflicting accounts of past events, cajoling reminiscences from older residents about people they used to work with or of places long since pulled down – there are bound to be mistakes. I may have mis-spelt a name or got a date wrong. For these, I apologize in advance. If you let me know they can be corrected in later editions.

Lastly, I've hugely enjoyed working on this project, mainly because of the help and encouragement of others. In effect, this book is a co-operative effort by residents of Southborough and High Brooms and it celebrates the towns they, and I, live in. My job has been to add the caption veg to the meat of the photographs to make it a complete meal. I hope you find it both tasty and satisfying.

Chris McCooey
June 1998

One
People

Southborough and High Brooms Welcome Club was set up in 1948 and used to meet every Wednesday in the Parochial Hall in Western Road (now demolished). The club was run jointly by the Toc H, the British Legion, Afternoon and Evening Townswomen's Guilds and St John's Methodist Church Women's Guild and then came under the aegis of the Old People's Welfare Committee, also known as Age Concern. This photograph was taken in the club's early years when rationing and austerity were still very much part of post-war life (note the newspaper table-cloths). Left to right, the ladies are: Mrs Smallcombe, Mrs Acott, Mrs Willard, Doris Raistrick, Mrs Bidwell, Mrs Hounsome, -?-. Past chairmen of the Welcome Club and Welfare Committee have included Mrs F.L. Cheesman (the first chairman of the club), Mrs I. Prue, Mrs M. Hounsome, Major E. Ruffell, Major Vic Liles, Ron King.

The annual seaside outing to Brighton or Hastings of the Southborough and High Brooms Welcome Club was a popular event that everybody looked forward to. The highlight for some was the traditional paddle in the sea. The ladies, left to right, are: Mrs Williams, Mrs Leney, Mrs Bryant, Mrs Hall, Mrs Wood, -?-, Mrs Styles.

In 1962 the Welcome Club had metamorphosed into Age Concern and the first bus was acquired in 1983. Left to right are: Dawn Mitchell (Day Centre organizer), Jenny Gudgin (Day Centre organizer), Jack Brightman, Harry Moody, Graham Lale (Help the Aged), Nancy Brown, Harry Dent, Ron King, Mary Moore, Sheila Barr (in wheelchair), Victor Liles, Wyn Kirkham, Mr Burchall, Lilian Crowther, Alice Wood, Ellen Hanmore, Florence Harris, Mrs Francis, Mabel Saunders, -?-, Doris Teagus, Mrs Colson, Doris Hewitt.

The Tworts came from a long line of Kent farmers and tanners. This is William, the father of Thomas who started the cricket-ball making business in Southborough. Thomas was quite a character – he was barely five feet tall and he attributed this lack of inches to the fact that his parents were first cousins and that his mother's parents (William Ballard and Susannah Twort) were first cousins too, although once removed. Thomas built a three storey house in Park Road after he had dissolved his partnership with Martin and moved his cricket-ball making business there in 1861. It was a family house with sixteen rooms and he called it 'Belle Vue' because it had a view of the Common. He planted his garden with apple, pear, plum, quince and cherry trees as well as a cob nut and walnut tree and a grape vine. He was zealous in the cause of temperance and would attend local fairs to sell soft drinks, displaying prominently a sign: SAMSON DRANK WATER AND REVIVED. He objected to the use of fermented drink in the administration of the Holy Sacrament and would walk to Bidborough to take Holy Communion there to avoid it. Another hobby was to make home-made fireworks – he was once summonsed before the local magistrates and charged with selling them without a licence, but was discharged with a warning.

Henry Crundwell was a leading member of Southborough society in the second half of the nineteenth century. He was chairman of the Local Board (in effect mayor to the town councillors) and in 1887 he missed only one of thirty-seven Board meetings (at this time, of course, women could neither stand for election nor vote). He was also the first chairman of Southborough Urban District Council from 1895 to 1897 and instrumental in setting up the Volunteer Fire Service. He was an enthusiastic cricketer and played for Southborough for many years. A farmer and business man he owned the tanyard for a number of years with his brother William. Henry had a son, also called Henry, but he predeceased his father when he died at the age of forty-seven in January 1891. Crundwell Road is named after the family.

Philip Hanmer was appointed town clerk in 1887 with a salary of £100 a year. He lived in Beulah Road, Tunbridge Wells. This photo was taken in 1901.

George Paine in 1902 when he was chairman of Southborough Tradesmen's Association. He later became chairman of Southborough Urban District Council from 1908 to 1910. Paine, Smith & Co. Ltd were bakers and confectioners and had three shops – one in Holden Park Road, one on the corner of Speldhurst Road and one on the Parade. He was a magistrate. His son, also called George, followed him into the family business and remembers delivering bread to the villages around Southborough by horse-drawn van. George Junior's proudest moment was when he was entrusted to take a horse and van for the first time on his own when he was twelve – the delivery of baker's yeast had failed to materialize and he was sent to the Kelsey Brewery in St John's Road to get two buckets of brewer's yeast.

John Carrick lived in London Road and was educated at the Holme Foundation School at the top of the Sceptre Hill. After leaving school he became a builder and set up his own firm. Sir David Salomons often employed him to carry out his plans for the Broomhill estate and Carrick was considered the baronet's right-hand man from whom he learned especially about metal and electricity work. He was a fine public servant, being the superintendent of the Fire Brigade, a member of the local Oddfellows Lodge and president of the Tradesmen's Association in 1891. A committed Christian, he attended Christ Church, sang in the choir and taught in the boys' Sunday school for the last eleven years of his life. A man of few words, he was nonetheless very well liked for his straightforwardness and the way he would help others. At his funeral in February 1893 his coffin was taken to the church on a fire engine drawn by two grey horses.

Arthur Pott was a wealthy businessman who had Bentham Hill House built to a design by Decimus Burton in 1831-32. He was High Sheriff of Kent at one time and made his money by the manufacturing of vinegar. Arthur Pott was Lord of the Manor of Southborough, a title he shared with John Deacon of Mabledon. When Arthur died in 1882, his brother Robert inherited it. Robert and his wife Anna had five children, one of whom was Robert Bertram Pott who fought in the Boer War. Robert Senior died in 1889 but his widow continued to live at Bentham Hill, which seems to have been the principal home of the family until the 1920s. The Potts were associated with the City Livery Company of Grocers since the middle of the seventeenth century and may have been important merchant traders for years before that – the family was awarded its coat of arms (which includes a collared and chained leopard) in 1583. The family motto was 'Fortis et arbutus' which means 'strong and evergreen'.

Robert Bertram Pott in 1931. An officer in the West Kent Yeomanry, he saw active service in the Boer War in 1899-1901 and in the First World War. The family owned Bentham Hill House. In 1928, Lt-Col. Pott (as he then was) married Vera, daughter of the late Sir John Henry and widow of Col. John Joseph O'Sullivan DSO. She brought with her a stepson for Bertram whose name (and voice) will be very familiar to many – Sir Peter O'Sullevan, the horse racing commentator. Peter remembers his stepfather with affection: 'a gentleman in all the best senses of the word'. In the First World War R.B. Pott served with the West Kent Yeomanry again at Gallipoli and in Egypt before being invalided home, ill. After the war he rode with the Eridge Hunt and won several point-to-point races. After Bentham Hill, he moved to Paveys in Speldhurst Road, Langton Green, then Little Royden near East Peckham. He died in November 1944 at Court Lodge, Frant.

Dr William Fairlie Clarke was a much-loved GP who served the people of Southborough for nine years until his early death in 1884 at fifty-one years of age. He was a founder member of the Working Men's Club and, although he was an active campaigner on behalf of the Church of England Temperance Society, he was happy for the club to make their own rules with regard to drink. The club in fact ruled that beer should be supplied to members who wanted it but they could have no more than a pint in the course of the evening. No other alcohol was allowed. Dr Clarke was elected to the Local Board, fulfilling the role of a town councillor today. At 'entertainments for the people', his readings and recitations were amusing and much appreciated. He also ran a Bible class for the young people of Southborough.

One day local doctor William Fairlie Clarke was summoned to a sick woman in a place that he had never heard of – a hamlet that had sprung up, inhabited by brickmakers and other workers. This, of course, was High Brooms and according to the book *Memoir of William Fairlie Clarke*, he at once realized that 'the people were in danger of lapsing into practical heathenism'. To counter this, he at once commenced a cottage Bible-reading once a week and conducted it himself for nine months. In 1881 he contracted typhoid fever and went to Ventnor on the Isle of Wight to recover. Three years later he was forced to give up work and died soon after, leaving four young sons without a father. The four oaks were planted beside the cricket pitch.

Mrs Annie Lawrence was the matron at the Isolation Hospital in Vauxhall Lane from 1911 to 1939 when it closed. George Paine, from the baking family, remembers as a child before the First World War being taken at night from his home in Holden Park Road in the 'fever van' to be treated by Mrs Lawrence for diphtheria. The van was drawn by horses stabled with Mr Shorter in Sheffield Road. After a month's stay with Mrs Lawrence, the seven-year-old boy walked back home. She is seen here wearing the Coronation Medal of King George VI.

Mr John Hook and Mrs Keziah Hook of 96 Springfield Road, some time between 1910 and 1920.

Henry Miles was pastor of the Bethel Baptist chapel in Western Road from 1903 to 1914. The building was built in 1882 and it is still used regularly for worship.

Alfred Burr had a local building and decorating business in Meadow Road. He was a leading light in the business community and was president in 1896 of the Southborough Traders' Association and also chairman between 1904 and 1906 of the Urban District Council which succeeded the Local Board. In the First World War he was a member of the Volunteer Force (equivalent to the Home Guard in the Second World War).

Kenneth Hutchings was born in Southborough on 7 December 1882, the youngest of four brothers, whose father was a GP with a surgery at 71 London Road. He went to Tonbridge School and was in the 1st XI for five years, the last two as captain. He played for Kent and toured with them to the United States in 1903. In the 1906 season he scored a century in each innings for Kent against Worcestershire. He went on to play for England and scored 126 in 125 minutes in the Second Test in Melbourne in Australia in January 1908 – England won by one wicket. He also played for Southborough on several occasions. Once he scored 138 in 42 minutes against United Banks – a correspondent reporting this match said he hit one six which went down the Hand and Sceptre chimney and came out of the front door! In November 1906 a dinner was held in his honour at the Victoria Hall and he recalled his early days in Southborough playing cricket in the garden of the family home – one afternoon seventeen window panes were broken! Known to everybody as 'Hutch', K.L. Hutchings was killed on the Western Front on 15 September 1916.

Park House on the corner of Park Road was built in Victorian times. During the First World War it was used as a convalescent home for wounded soldiers. In 1922 the Royal Antediluvian Order of Buffaloes acquired it and it became an orphanage. This photo records the arrival of the first two boys who are being greeted by Mr and Mrs Sealey who ran the orphanage. Mr Sealey, in the white trousers, was an ex-Cavalry man and was at one time the trumpeter to Lord Kitchener. The little boy on the right is Arthur Pope and like many orphans went on to join the military after leaving the home. In 1935 he was a bandsman in the Royal West Kents in India. After the Second World War, the house became a Kent County Council children's reception centre, but was demolished in the 1970s and residential houses were built on the site.

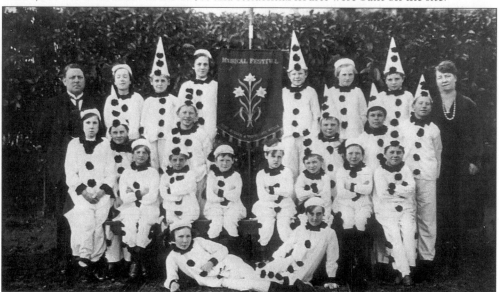

Choristers of the Buffalo Orphanage win the Courthope Challenge Banner in the Tunbridge Wells Music Festival of 1929. The clowns' costumes were used year after year and the choir was called 'The Clutch and Gearbox Pierrots'.

The Bell Inn Cork Club, July 1926. The members of the club had to produce a cork from their pocket if challenged by another member, otherwise they were fined. The large man seated in the middle of the front row is the landlord Percy John Buckland and on his right is William Buckland. Of the others, left to right, standing at the back: Hodge, Diplock, -?-, Rodwell (the town's lamplighter), -?-, Chatfield, -?-, -?-, John (a German working at the Bell). The only other known persons: in the next row standing third from the left is Claud Bending and the sailor sitting at the front on the left is Morley. The darker of the two dogs at the front on the left was called Bromley.

Teaching staff of St Peter's Boys' School in the early 1920s. Left to right, front row: Miss Capon, Miss Nellie Cox (daughter of the headmaster), Miss Cockerall. Back row: Mr George Bocking ('a tyrant'), Mr Williams (temporary and 'very Welsh'), Mr Clift, Mr W.F.A. Cox.

The staff of Holden House, *c.* 1935. Left to right, back row: George Crust (chauffeur), Fred Smith (second gardener), Bob Belton (garden boy), Ernest Fitch (houseman), Joyce Edna Stevenson (schoolgirl), Sidney Stevenson (head gardener). Middle row, seated: Doris Crust, Doris Pope (parlour maid), Ethel (kitchen maid), Ethel Hudgell (cook), Clara Fitch (maid), Edna Stevenson. Front row, children: Gordon Crust, Alfred Hudgell, Kenneth Fitch.

Mr P.A. Godfrey Phillips, always known as Phil, owned Holden House from 1948 to his death in 1983. He joined the RAF during the war and ended up a squadron leader. He was chairman and managing director of the family tobacco business before it was sold. He was District Commissioner for Scouts for many years and liked to watch the cricket on the Common. A keen gardener, the grounds of Holden House were opened every year in aid of the RNLI. Phil owned an Aston Martin and his enthusiastic driving both thrilled and terrified his passengers.

Lt-Col. Frank Harris, although he lived in Bidborough, served on many committees and contributed greatly to the community as a sportsman as well. He was a member of Southborough Cricket Club for more than seventy-five years and president for the last thirteen years of his life. He died in 1957 at the age of ninety-two. He first played for Southborough in 1881 and in that year in one match he clean bowled the famous Tom Pawley with his third ball – Pawley went on to captain England and took a Test side to Australia in the early 1900s. In a Centenary Match played on the Common against Ashurst in July 1938, Frank came out of retirement at the age of seventy-three to take three wickets for five runs in six overs, three of which were maidens. Each side fielded fifteen players and Southborough won by 88 runs, scoring 173 to their opponents' 85. His grave is beside the seat in Bidborough churchyard.

Group Captain George Darley, who lives in Southborough, spent twenty-six years in the RAF. In June 1940 (when this photo was taken) he was appointed to command 609 Squadron, a fighter unit. He devised a way of fighting which was very successful during the Battle of Britain. He taught his pilots the art of deflection shooting on a curving attack, avoiding the fire of rear gunners and 'aiming at the front office where the pilot was, so the aircraft didn't get back to France with a dead rear gunner – it didn't get back at all.' When he left 609 Squadron four months later, promoted to Wing Commander, he and his men had shot down eighty-five enemy aircraft. After the war he was twice station commander at RAF West Malling before retiring in 1958.

John and Eileen Rabbitt outside their pub, The Beehive, in Modest Corner. The Rabbitts ran the pub from 1955 to 1983 when John died and Eileen retired. It was much appreciated for its homely coal fires and warm welcome. John's ringing of a handbell and calling of 'Time, Gentlemen, Please' in a sergeant major's voice left nobody in any doubt when it was closing time. In the summer the front garden was a riot of colour with annuals and bedding plants. Speldhurst sausages were a speciality for a snack at lunch time.

Two
Buildings
and
Streets

The Parade of shops at the north end of London Road in the 1920s.

Paine Smith was a steam bakery in Holden Park Road. George Paine was a well known Southborough man who founded the business in the late nineteenth century. His son, also called George, was born in Eugenie Cottage, the house next to the shop, and remembers delivering the bread by horse-drawn cart to the surrounding villages. The bakery's selling slogan was 'The Bread is Always the Same'. The shop was Beeline Taxis in recent years but is now empty.

The Bell Inn, London Road, was run by B. Baker of Tonbridge, before it was leased to F. Leney & Son of Wateringbury for £120 per annum in 1892. One landlord was fined 5s in 1897 for selling adulterated gin. Frederick Tanner came to the Bell in 1911 after running the Junction at Groombridge. He was an avid football fan and did a lot for the local teams, especially helping to introduce the game to youngsters. He died after falling into a diabetic coma in January 1924, aged only forty-nine and so Southborough lost a popular landlord and a much valued figure in local sports.

An aerial view of London Road from above the Hand and Sceptre Hotel looking south in 1955. In the foreground on the left is a field that used to be rented for grazing sheep by Sid White, the local butcher whose shop was on the corner of London Road and Still Lane opposite. The field is now the Pennington Grounds. The lock-up garages beside the petrol pumps (the Shell garage today) can be seen on the corner of London Road and behind it is a large white house on the site of Southborough Hall; this has been pulled down to make way for the doctors' surgery, St Andrew's Medical Centre.

Southfields was the big house in its own grounds which stretched along the London Road from Yew Tree Road to Powder Mill Lane. It was the home of Frank Weare, son of the founder of the High Brooms Brick and Tile Company in the early 1900s. The house was pulled down after the grounds were sold to the Local Education Authority in 1929; the grounds are now the Skinners' School sports field.

The general store on the corner of Edward Street and Springfield Road sometime before the Second World War. It finally stopped being a corner shop in the 1980s and was converted into the front room of a house in 1998.

Edgar Clark Savidge ran this off-licence in Church Road until 1922. From 1843 to 1875 the building housed the local post office. In the 1950s it was run by Harry V. Tranter and was known as 'Tranters'. It is now an antiques shop. The house on the left has been a restaurant for some years and is now called 'Right on the Green'.

Holden House was built in the late eighteenth century and for a time was the parsonage to St Peter's after the church was built in 1830. It was a private house up until the death in 1983 of the last owner, the tobacco millionaire Mr P.A. Godfrey Phillips. Much of the land was sold off for building but the formal gardens closest to the house remain. It is now a residential home.

The Beehive was originally only licensed to sell beer which was brewed in Modest Corner by Robert John Phipps who set up in business in 1857 in the building that fronts Victoria Road (it ceased brewing in 1895). When the landlord, Stephen Smith, took over in 1873, Superintendent Dance of the Tonbridge police told the licensing magistrates that 'the house had now got a very bad name.' The court told Smith that he must strive to improve its reputation or else the licence would be revoked. This is in fact what happened 122 years later when immediate neighbours made so many complaints that renewal of the licence was refused and the pub is now a private house. This photograph was taken about 1900; the pub is on the left and the two other cottages have been pulled down. The lady is Mrs Carter, mother of the blacksmith in Forge Road, William Carter, and great grandmother of Alec Brown, former cricket ball maker, who lives at 13 Holden Corner.

The Pound for stray animals was located on a detached part of the Common on the east side of London Road between Vauxhall Lane and Birchwood Garage (the house named 'The Pound' is on the site). The first 'street driver' (whose duty was to impound stray cattle and other animals) was John Knight and he was appointed in 1773. By 1810 the street driver needed two assistants as the area covered included Tunbridge Wells. The fee to release impounded animals varied: horses and cattle were a shilling each, five sheep or fewer cost sixpence and five hogs or fewer cost a shilling. Street drivers were employed up until the First World War.

An aerial view looking north-west across London Road in 1925. Gallards Close (in the foreground) was built in 1912 and financed by the C.J. Ballard Charitable Trust. This was established in 1906 by a retired builder who lived in Boyne Park, Tunbridge Wells, and left £37,000 in his will. From this legacy, £5,000 was allocated to cover the purchase of land and the houses' construction costs. The Close was built to provide accommodation for four married couples, eight single men and eight single women. When the first residents moved in they were given a bedstead and a supply of coal. They had to be over fifty-five, have lived in the area for a while and able to look after themselves. Back then, the residents were called inmates and one of the rules was that no women were allowed to live with the male inmates in their single residences. However, in 1932 a Mr Wood flouted the rules more than once and was asked to leave, the only resident to date forced to do so.

The idea for a hall was first mooted at a dinner of the Southborough Tradesmen's Association in December 1896 when the discussions turned to how best to celebrate Queen Victoria's Diamond Jubilee. Sir David Salomons contributed £3,000 of the total cost of £5,000. In a letter to the Local Board, Sir David had pointed out that it was important that the local people not only use the hall but look after it: 'When a poor man was given a horse he was most grateful for the gift but forgot that it required feeding afterwards.' Sir David was not an advocate of indiscriminate charity and had a keen sense for humbug and charlatanism. In effect, the Royal Victoria Hall became the first municipal hall in Great Britain. This photograph shows the original façade before it was changed in 1977. There was controversy over the renovation of the hall; opinion was divided between those who wanted to preserve it as 'a gem of Victorian art' and those that thought it looked like 'the façade of a Welsh Baptist chapel'.

Powdermill Lane got its name from the manufacture of gunpowder. Being fairly isolated, the mills quite often blew up, it was a good place to carry on this activity, away from habitation. There were at least two mills – Old Forge and Brokes – which both changed to gunpowder manufacturing after the decline of the iron industry in the eighteenth century. Old Forge changed to gunpowder manufacturing in 1771. It was a pestle mill and very dangerous to operate as the volatile ingredients were compounded in mortars, the pestles being driven up and down by a water wheel. It was one of the few mills in the country that made the extra fine powder used for fowling pieces but an explosion in 1774 necessitated the rebuilding of the mill. Competition from the Leigh powder mills near Tonbridge forced the mills to change to corn grinding sometime in the first half of the nineteenth century.

Forge Farm in Powdermill Lane taken in 1910. Today it is an abattoir. The oast house suggests hops were grown on the farm and the chickens and cows would certainly have been sufficient to keep the family in eggs and milk.

Southborough Hall in 1828. This was on the site of St Andrew's Medical Centre and is not to be confused with the Old Hall (which was not old but built sometime in the middle of the nineteenth century) which was pulled down to provide a site for Pinewood Court.

Stuart Cottage, London Road is one of the oldest houses in Southborough, probably built for a yeoman farmer sometime in the sixteenth century. At first it stood at right angles to the road with the entrance on the south side; at a later date wings were added and the main door made to face the main road. Early this century it was two or even three cottages but now it is a single private house and restored inside to its Tudor original (three later fireplaces were removed to uncover the original made of Kentish ragstone with two escutcheons). The snowdrift is thought to have occurred sometime in the 1920s.

SOUTHBOROUGH COMMON.

Particulars and Conditions of Sale

OF THE

HIGHLY VALUABLE

FREEHOLD PROPERTY,

KNOWN AS

'THE TANNERY,'

HOLDEN ROAD,

Embracing an area of about

— 8a. 3r. 28p. —

For over a century used as a Tannery, and having

ALL NECESSARY BUILDINGS FOR A LARGE TRADE.

A SPLENDID SUPPLY OF SOFT WATER.

It forms an exceptionally valuable

BUILDING ESTATE

Facing the far-famed Common, with long frontages to the Holden, Prospect and Tannery Roads.

The Valuable Machinery may be taken or not at the option of the Purchaser.

MESSRS.

DENYER & COLLINS

Are favoured with instructions from the Mortgagees to SELL by AUCTION, at the

Swan Hotel, Tunbridge Wells,

On FRIDAY, OCTOBER 25th, 1912,

At FOUR o'clock precisely.

Particulars, Plan and Conditions of Sale of the

Solicitors:	Auctioneers:
Messrs. STENNING, KNOCKER & THOMPSON, Tonbridge and Headcorn.	Messrs. DENYER & COLLINS, Tunbridge Wells, Tonbridge, and 16, Abchurch Lane, E.C.

Notice for the auction of the Tannery to be held on 25 October 1912 and sold as building land. The plot consisted of just over eight acres between Tanyard Lane, Holden Road, Vale Road and Prospect Road. The smaller tannery, which was adjacent and known as the White Heather Tanyard, continued until 1922.

This photograph was taken just before the Second World War. The library had been a Temperance Hotel in 1871, then a coffee tavern and after that a stationer's. The street lamps are gas. The Royal Victoria Hall is on the right. The idea for the hall (as well as three fifths of its cost) came from Sir David Salomons of Broomhill. He proposed to the Southborough Council in 1897 (Queen Victoria's Jubilee year, hence its name) that a hall be constructed for the benefit of the people. This came about because he was somewhat annoyed by the attitude of the local vicar who refused permission for the Parochial Hall to be used for certain public activities.

Ormonde Lodge gatehouse was part of the Mabledon estate when it was owned by the Deacon family in the first half of the twentieth century. John Deacon, who died in 1941 without marrying, had two sisters, Jane and Beatrice, and Fosse Bank on Quarry Hill and Ormonde Lodge in Southborough had been earmarked by the Deacons as the family home of the two sisters when they got married, but neither of them ever did. It was pulled down about 1936 when the Barnardo's home was built, but the gatehouse remained until 1965 when it too was pulled down. Captain Meadows, himself a Barnardo's boy, had left money in his will and this was used to help finance the new school, hence the name, Meadows School, today.

An old map of Southborough showed a cock horse stable on the pumping station site where Victoria Road becomes Bentham Hill. A cock horse was necessary to assist a team of horses dragging a heavy load up a steep hill. Laws governed the number of horses which could be hitched to various types of cart, as overloading had seriously damaged the unmetalled roads. The pumping station was built in 1885 and finally closed in 1973 when it was converted into a private house.

There used to be a pond on the corner of Pennington Road and London Road opposite the Imperial Hotel, as can be seen here. In 1871, the Local Board was asked if the 'stagnant pond in the principal thoroughfare of Southborough could be filled in because it was prejudicial to the health of inhabitants and visitors complained of its obnoxious emanations as it was made the receptacle of all sorts of rubbish and the decomposing bodies of dead animals were often seen floating on its surface'. The Lords of the Manor prevented this by claiming that it was used by cattle for drinking purposes. Carts were often left standing in the pond to swell the spokes of their wooden wheels that summer heat had caused to shrink and rattle. In 1881 the Southborough Local Board had to give notice to various people to cease using the water from the pond to wash carriages. The chapel on the right was for the Wesleyans and was built in 1871 at a cost of £950. This became too small and was pulled down, to be replaced with the existing building just a few hundreds further along London Road. This new Methodist church was built in 1936-37 and cost £10,000.

St Peter's on the Common was consecrated on 25 August 1830 and in those days had a tower with no spire (one was added in 1866). Tickets to the consecration service informed that 'collections will be made at the door for the purpose of building a schoolhouse contiguous to the church'. It was built because Southborough's approximate 700 population at that time had no place to worship and few made the effort to travel on a Sunday to churches in Bidborough, Tonbridge or Tunbridge Wells. Decimus Burton designed the church and the total cost was £8,436. The main contributors were local landowners and businessmen: Mr Deacon, Mr Broadley Wilson (who lived in Ormonde Lodge and whose wife presented the communion plate) and Mr Crundwell. The first vicar was the Revd John Tucker who had been the curate at nearby Bidborough. He resigned in 1833 when he went as a chaplain to India.

The Weavers was known as Stemps or Dudeneys Farm, named after the farmers who lived here. A cowshed used to stand on the corner of Doric Avenue and the fields stretched away behind it. The thatched building was known as Wynne's Cake Shoppe. In Victorian times the building was tile hung but the original Tudor woodwork was revealed again when Mr Bridges bought the house in 1926. It became the Weavers Tea Room in 1930 and is a restaurant today.

The interior of the Weavers, showing the very high roofed room built on the back of the building. It is believed that it was constructed like this so that the looms of the Huguenot weavers could be accommodated, hence the name of the restaurant today. Weaving was an important industry in Tonbridge when Southborough was just that: the South Borough of Tonbridge parish.

A chalybeate spring rises underneath the Weavers. When it was a farm the spring water was used to cool the churns used for the cows' milk. The spring flowed into the back garden and visitors could take the water just like they could at the more famous spring on the Pantiles in Tunbridge Wells. Below the spring were watercress beds and one old resident of Southborough interviewed by the late Doug Bennett remembers being paid by a local doctor to get leeches from these beds.

There was a chalybeate spring in the garden of 1 Doric Avenue which was probably from the same water source as the one in the Weavers. Up until the Second World War visitors to Southborough and locals could drink the water or take it away free of charge by kind permission of the owner, Mr Parker.

Stidolph Brothers' Emporium stood at the top of Victoria Road (on the site of Cosack House). The business had been founded in 1799 and included a wine and spirits merchant, a bakery, a family grocery and a drapery. The brothers had a tea and Italian warehouse and a second shop at Brightridge in Southborough. They also ran an undertaking business and advertised 'funerals economically conducted to all parts of the Kingdom.' According to a fulsome advertising write-up around the turn of the century, 'the several shops contain splendid stocks of great magnitude and variety.'

Mr J. S. Norrie was a member of the Pharmaceutical Society. In 1889 the shop had been the premises of a photographer called Tester and a stationer and printer called Cane. In 1892 it was a chemist and the owner's name was Chantry (today it is a pet shop). This photograph was taken in 1911 when the shop was decorated to celebrate the Coronation of King George V and Queen Mary.

London Road has always been an important shopping street – in 1889 there were seven grocery shops and seven butchers' shops on the western side between Speldhurst Road and Victoria Road as well as a bank (Hodgkins and Beeching), three drapers, two boot and shoemakers, a fancy stationer, two corn chandlers, a tobacconist, a tailor, a dressmaker, a watchmaker, a fishmonger and a baker. This is the north end of Southborough looking along the Parade – note the open-top bus with an advert for Noakes (still going strong) in Tunbridge Wells.

The Isolation Hospital in Vauxhall Lane is now Moatenden, breeding and boarding kennels. Following an outbreak of smallpox in Tonbridge in 1878 Mr (later Sir Julian) Goldsmid granted permission for an isolation hospital to be built on his land at the Tonbridge end of Vauxhall Lane (this is now the Cottage Hospital, formerly the Queen Victoria Hospital) and it was opened in 1879. The Local Board was hopeful that residents of Southborough – if they had the misfortune to contract smallpox, diphtheria, cholera or scarlet fever – could be treated in the hospital too, but a letter to Sir Julian Goldsmid in 1881 with this request was answered unfavourably. It said: 'it appears that ere long Southborough will become part of Tunbridge Wells and it would be a far more natural arrangement that Southborough should combine with Tunbridge Wells for the treatment of infectious diseases.' This prompted a search for a suitable site in or around Southborough. Sites in Bidborough and Powdermill Lane were suggested but there was considerable local opposition from neighbouring residents. Eventually in 1893 a compulsory purchase order was obtained for land owned by Sir Julian in Vauxhall Lane and less than a mile from the Tonbridge isolation hospital. A loan of £3,500 was raised and the buildings were erected and declared ready for patients in August 1895. Edward and Ellen Maynard of High Brooms were appointed as attendant and nurse respectively of the Isolation Hospital in Vauxhall Lane. Part of the attendant's job was 'not to permit wines or spirits or other intoxicating liquors of any kind to be brought into the hospital' and to 'disinfect all articles of clothing and bedding which may be in use in the hospital' and to keep 'the paths and walks free from weeds and the grounds in good order.' John Taylor of No. 1 Meadow Road provided an ambulance for £42 10s 0d and Mr E.G. Miles was hired to provide a horse and to take patients to the hospital as and when required for a fee of 4s if the patient lived in Southborough and 5s if they lived in High Brooms. Uniforms for staff cost £4 10s 0d. The hospital closed in October 1939.

Southborough Lodge was owned by Mrs Blackburn Maze and it stood on the corner of Speldhurst Road and London Road. There was an animal and pet graveyard in the garden. A small village grew up around this part of Southborough and it was called Nonesuch Green. Today the house on the corner of Speldhurst Road and Charles Street is called Nonesuch House.

The Crown Inn, London Road, being rebuilt in 1907. Drinking after hours appears to have been a feature of the pub. When the publican Hilton William Read, always known as 'Jack', kept the pub in the 1970s, he always told the police that he was helping to celebrate his dog's birthday when they came at midnight to see why people were still drinking. At one time, local police pointed out that his dog had had seven birthdays in one year. Jack had been a music-hall master of ceremonies and wrote a book on the subject *Empires, Hippodromes and Palaces*. He also used to write scripts for the Tunbridge Wells Revue Society. When he took over the Crown in 1973, Jack served his Whitbread beer through top-gas pressure pumps. He found an old beer engine in his cellar and started to serve beer with this hand-pump. Sales from the pressure beer went from twenty barrels a week to one while the hand-pump beer went in the other direction. The brewery complained and tried to enforce pressure-pump sales but the customers complained in their turn and set up a 'Free Range Charter' – this was before the Campaign for Real Ale (CAMRA) had really got going. As a result of Jack's stance, within six months all local Whitbread pubs could sell hand-pumped beer if they wished.

Three
Events and Celebrations

Queen Victoria's Golden Jubilee in 1887 was celebrated in Southborough by a holiday, planting an oak on the Common, a dinner for old people and a tea for children. There were also sports events with prizes and the day was finished off by a grand fireworks display. The dinner and tea committee accepted a tender from the Coffee Tavern (the old Temperance Hotel, now the Sub Aqua shop) in Southborough to provide roast and boiled beef, mutton, vegetables, salad, pickles, plum pudding, bread and cheese, lemonade and ginger beer for 2s a head. The committee was pleased that the provisions would all be obtained from local tradesmen and allowed one pint of mild ale to the males and a half pint of the same to the females 'if desired'. The tea for the girls and infants under six was held on the Common at 4 p.m. and the boys' tea followed at 5 p.m. The tender for that was also accepted from the Coffee Tavern at 5d per head and the children got tea, cake, bread and butter, and bread and jam. To pay for the day's celebrations subscriptions were solicited – Mr J. Deacon of Mabledon gave the most, £25, followed by Sir J Goldsmid of Summerhill with £10 and the High Brooms Brick Company five guineas. Fifty more people donated between £5 and a guinea. There was enough money left over to buy a first-class fire escape (named 'the Jubilee') for the local fire brigade which was made by E.H. Bayley & Co. of Southwark and cost £55 19s 0d.

The Diamond Jubilee of Queen Victoria in 1897 was marked throughout the length and breadth of Great Britain and Ireland and all over the Empire by celebrations, new public buildings, and the manufacture of all manner of medals, mugs, jugs and artefacts with the stern queen's head on them. In High Brooms, the brickworks fired a special plaque using the local Wadhurst clay and is now seen on a house in Forge Road. The most important countries of the Empire are recorded – Canada, Australia, New Zealand, Burmah (*sic*), Africa, West Indies, Gibraltar, Malta, Cyprus, Egypt – as is the fact that Victoria was also Empress of India.

A special holiday was declared throughout the land on 22 June 1897 for Queen Victoria's Diamond Jubilee, and the High Brooms Brick and Tile Works had their own celebrations. The company gave a special dinner to the workmen, their wives and tenants at 12 noon, then at 2 p.m. all the inhabitants gathered in Gordon Road and marched to the sports field where they sang the National Anthem. From 2.30 p.m. there were general sports races including a blindfold wheelbarrow race and an egg and ladle race – first prize for each was 7s 6d, second prize 5s, third prize 2s 6d. There was a race for women over fifty years – the first prize for this was a new dress to the value of £1. There were special races for brick company employees only and there were juvenile races for boys and girls under fifteen years of age including a 'jingling race' with the proviso that the winner of two races was ineligible to take any other. At 3.30 p.m. there was a dinner for old people (over fifty years of age), followed by tea for children of three to fifteen years. Mrs F. Weare (wife of the owner) distributed the prizes at 6.30 p.m. and at 7.30 p.m. the dancing began. During the day the Electric Temperance Band performed, with Mr Slaughter conducting.

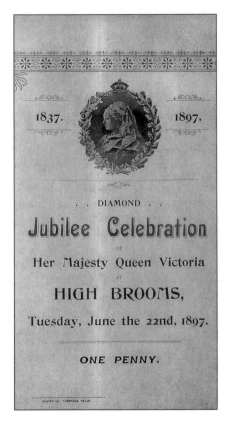

1837.   1897.

. . DIAMOND . .

Jubilee Celebration

OF

Her Majesty Queen Victoria

AT

HIGH BROOMS,

Tuesday, June the 22nd, 1897.

ONE PENNY.

Sir David Salomons (centre, holding the hat) and the members of the Urban District Council at the opening of the Royal Victoria Hall on 17 January 1900. The first events were two patriotic concerts for the Transvaal War Fund. Everybody in the photograph, except the two on the left at the back, has some form of facial hair as was the fashion at that time. Sir David was instrumental in getting the hall built because he wanted a hall for the people of Southborough with fewer restrictions on its use than at the Parochial Hall.

Public reception for Captain R.B. Pott of the West Kent Yeomanry, who lived at Bentham Hill House, to celebrate his safe return from the Boer War in July 1901. Vice chairman of the District Council, H.R. Brown, and fellow councillors are welcoming him home outside the town offices in London Road. After the speeches, the captain was driven along London Road to the Common and then to Bentham Hill to greet his widowed mother in the house.

Maypole dancing on the cricket pitch on the Common to celebrate the coronation of Edward VII in 1902. Miss Cook, the headmistress of St Peter's Girls' School, used to organize maypole dancing every year but this was stopped by the vicar of St Peter's who considered it an unsuitable recreation for young girls.

High Brooms Brick and Tile Company workers dressed in their best suits, ready for an outing, in 1911. The company was founded in 1885 by John Smith Weare and three generations of Weares ran the company before it was forced to close, because of a building slump, in 1968. The Weares were very much respected by the employees, who were housed by the company and looked after financially, socially and spiritually. In the first year of trading the company declared a dividend of 7.5 per cent on its ordinary stock. The founder loaned a hall to his workers in 1887 and the High Brooms Working Men's Club was formed (it is still going strong) and he gave land so that a mission hall could be built. Regular outings and sports days helped keep good relations between employer and his workers (over 500 worked for the company at its peak).

Hospital Sunday at Southborough 2-7-22.

The Hospital Sunday Parade was an annual event that raised money for local good causes. The parade usually started at Yew Tree Road and then went up and down the streets to the west of London Road and then from Springfield Road along London Road to Park Road before joining Pennington Road and up Church Road to the Common where an open-air service was held. After the service it returned along London Road to the Royal Victoria Hall where tea was served to those taking part. These included the Southborough Fire Brigade, neighbouring village bands, the Rusthall Cadets of Temperance, the Equitable Friendly Society, the National Deposit Friendly Society, the Oddfellows and the Ancient Order of Foresters. Notice the long poles; these in fact were pipes which were held over collecting buckets so that people watching from first and second floor windows could give money. This was the parade in July 1922 and the horse-drawn decorated cart carries the parade queen and her attendants. The parades continued until the introduction of the National Health Service in 1948.

This is the annual outing of the Bell Inn Cork Club in 1927. The pub had a reputation as a 'widow maker' – the wives of four publicans took over the tenancy (albeit briefly) after their husbands' deaths while 'on duty'. The Cork Club members had to carry a cork with them at all times. If challenged by another member, at any time, and found without a cork they were fined.

F. Waters' greengrocery at 3 Bedford Road bedecked with bunting to celebrate the Silver Jubilee of George V in 1935. Fanny Waters took over running the family business when her husband William went off to fight in the First World War. Their son, George, left school early on account of asthma; he helped and subsequently went on to develop his own wholesale business from a warehouse in Norton Road. William, Fanny's husband, was knocked down by a car outside the Bell Inn in Southborough and was taken to the General Hospital in Tunbridge Wells where he died the following day, 6 December 1931. At the inquest a verdict of 'accidental death' was recorded with no blame attached to the driver, Albert John Pitkin, a chauffeur driving his employer's family back to London. The Waters family insist William had popped into the pub for 'just the one', having gone out with the intention of getting a piece of steak for his dinner. His son, George, remarked after the inquest: 'And we never even found the steak.' Was William Waters the first person from Southborough to die in a road accident?

The coronation of King George VI and Queen Elizabeth was celebrated on 12 May 1937. The celebrations committee, under the chairmanship of the head of the Urban District Council, W.H. Fleming JP, drew up a full programme which began with ringing the bells of St Peter's at 8 a.m. and ended with fireworks and a bonfire at 10 p.m. In an ominous portent of what was to come, the 314th (Kent) Anti-Aircraft Searchlight Company, Royal Engineers, lit up the night sky with a tattoo of beams. During the day was a carnival procession with four classes: decorated commercial vehicles (they included 'Key to the Empire' 'Southborough Fanciers' and 'New Zealand Produce'), decorated private vehicles ('The Crown', 'Crazy Knuts' Band'), decorated bicycles and turnouts ('The Ship's in Port Again', 'Miss Daffodil') and fancy costumes ('Charlie Chaplin', 'Telephone and Pillar Box' and 'An Owl'). There was a fun fair with games such as Aunt Sally, Bursting the Beacons, Tilting the Bucket and a Punch and Judy show and all children could have a free tea near St Peter's.

Coronation
of Their Majesties

**KING GEORGE VI. and
QUEEN ELIZABETH**

12th May, 1937

SOUTHBOROUGH COMMON   *(Reproduced by permission of Messrs. André Page & Co.)*

Souvenir Programme
of the
Southborough Celebrations

(Published by the Southborough Celebrations Committee, Council Offices, Southborough).

PRICE - - THREE PENCE

The end of the Second World War was celebrated all over the UK after Germany surrendered on 9 May 1945 and Japan three months later, on 14 August. Thousands of street parties were held, including this one for children in Nursery Road, High Brooms. The man standing by the kerb on the left is George Frederick Kew.

This is the family butcher's shop of E.T. Quinnell in Colebrook Road, High Brooms, decorated to celebrate the end of the Second World War. This came on 14 August 1945 when Japan acknowledged defeat (note the Rising Sun flag in the window) after two atomic bombs were dropped on Hiroshima and Nagasaki.

Street party on 9 May 1945 in Castle Street and Sheffield Road. The lady on the right is Ivy Willcocks (wife of Jack, the Southborough goalkeeper). The lady third from right is Mrs Willcocks, mother of Jack. The fifth from right is Mrs Plumridge. The small boy in the front in black with white collar is Michael Willcocks, son of Ivy, and immediately behind him is Mr Webster with Betty Willcocks (Ivy's eldest daughter) on his left. The man second from the left at the top is Mr Plumridge and third from the left is Percy Tingley.

This is a celebratory dinner held by the Civil Defence in the Royal Victoria Hall, just after the Second World War ended in August 1945. The lady on the left, turning round, is Mrs Weekes of Holden Corner – the only other persons known in this row are the young man, second from the right, who is the son of the lady next to him, Mrs Norrie. In the second row, left to right are Mrs Edna Stevenson (née Dedman), and next to her is Mr Sidney Stevenson who both lived at Holden House Cottages. Sitting along the same row, five and six from the left, are Mr Norrie and his daughter Peggy.

Commemorating sixty years in business of the baking company Paine Smith in 1948. Left to right, back row: Percy Puttock (driver), Eddie Dear (foreman in the cake bakery), Mrs Waghorn (shop assistant), Mrs Tingley (assistant), Miss Lavender (shop assistant), Mr Hubble (roundsman), Jim, Cyril Dann (baker), -?-, David Bennet (pastry maker, one of triplets), Sid Hickmott (dough maker), Fred Bowles (baker). Second row from back: Mr Goodwin (bread baker), Miss Fisk, Mrs Everest (roundswoman), Mrs Rose Page (shop assistant), Thomas Sprague (roundsman), Frederick Barnaby (deputy foreman), Mr Hemsley, Frederick Webb (foreman and driver), Ronald Waghorn (driver), David Baird (confectioner), Harry Daniels (master baker), Joseph Saunders (foreman), George Waghorn (mechanic). Third row: Mr A. Williams (roundsman), Mr Wylie (roundsman), Miss Winifred Spray, Doris Wilson (office), Toni Andrews (office), Mrs Florence Smallcombe, Jill Groves (assistant), -?-, -?-, Rose Cottenham (driver), Ron Baldock, Frederick Baldock, Dennis Acott (confectioner). Front row: Miss Dorothy 'Dot' Turley (assistant and petrol pump attendant), Miss Summerfield (cook), Roy Fox (manager), Miss Hards (director), George Paine (owner), Miss Edwards (office), Miss Kathleen Tilly Wood, -?-.

The coronation of Queen Elizabeth II on 2 June 1953 was celebrated in Southborough by the erection of a decorated arch by Mr R.N. Carr and members of the Southborough Trade and Improvement Association. There was a carnival procession which made its way to the Common where there was a fireworks display at 9.30 p.m. Following that, Miss Southborough, Rosemary Churn, accompanied by her maids of honour, Madeleine Cook and Helene Knowles, lit the bonfire on the green and dancing commenced. Other events were the presentation of a New Testament to all children up to school leaving age (the Council still has about thirty of these bibles). The next day private car owners took the old folks on a drive to Mereworth.

Prince Philip visited Southborough in 1964 to attend a charity function at Beth Holme Holiday Home, in Church Road. He arrived by helicopter and landed in the field beside London Road – today it is the Pennington Road Grounds (Southborough Cricket Club had refused permission for the Royal helicopter to land on the cricket pitch). The prince was met by Alf Francis, the mayor of Southborough, and his wife, who escorted them the short distance to the home. The view is from Pennington Road, in front of G. Hayden, the greengrocer's, and is looking towards Stuart Cottage.

Four
Transport

This two-horse trap was used by Mrs Sarah Isabella Harland, a member of the ship-building family, who lived at Great Bounds from 1896 to 1925. The man standing is believed to be Mr Tutchner. The photograph was taken in London Road outside what is now the fireplace shop.

This is the kiln constructed on Forge Farm in Powdermill Lane to make the bricks used in building the Colebrook Viaduct. The line between Tonbridge and Tunbridge Wells was opened in 1845. There was no station on the line until the Southborough station was opened in 1893. This station's name was changed in 1925 to High Brooms. The High Brooms Brick and Tile Company had its own sidings off the Tonbridge to Tunbridge Wells line so that the bricks could be loaded straight onto the wagons.

The Colebrook Viaduct was constructed between 1844 and 1845 when a branch line was built to connect Tonbridge with Tunbridge Wells. The line had to diverge nearly at right angles from the main line and go through a tunnel so that Somerhill Park could be avoided. The line was opened on 21 September 1845 and the first to travel its length were directors of the railway and guests in a train of four engines and twenty-six carriages, flying flags and decked with wild flowers of the season. The major engineering feat of the five-mile line was the construction of the 254-yard-long viaduct, which has twenty-six arches. This photograph was taken in 1970 and the engine is a Class 4 (2-6-4) Tank, which were built from 1951 onwards.

Nell's Bridge on the line between High Brooms Station and Colebrook Viaduct. Old Forge Farm can be seen in the middle distance. The brickbridge has now been replaced by a metal pedestrian bridge.

A steamroller built in 1892 and used to haul gravel from the pit on Southborough Common.

This steam-driven vehicle was used by Southborough removal contractors J. Martin & Sons whose offices used to be in London Road on the corner with Still Lane.

The High Brooms Brick and Tile Company was in business between 1885 and 1968. Bricks for projects abroad (they were used in the construction of the Aswan Dam in Egypt, for example) or elsewhere in the UK were despatched by rail but, if they were being used locally, then they would be delivered by lorry. This steam wagon, built in 1928 by Richard Garrett & Sons of Leiston, Suffolk, was delivered new to the company and was in service until 1934 when it was taken off the road following steep increases in road fund taxation for steam vehicles, ostensibly to compensate for the fact that their fuel was untaxed.

Farrant's are still in business in High Brooms. The haulage contracting business was founded by George E. Farrant (1865-1943) at premises in Colebrook Road about the time of his marriage in 1888. The company had a number of steam vehicles, including this one for haulage. The first steam vehicle was bought in 1910, a B2 type five-ton steam tractor built by W Tasker & Son Ltd of Andover, Hants. In 1914 while driving one of these tractors, a wheel came off on Quarry Hill and the vehicle turned over. The steersman was thrown clear but died of his injuries and George Farrant was trapped by his right leg. It was so badly broken that it had to be amputated at the knee. Steam engines needed water and if the haulage contract took the vehicle to London the route had to be chosen carefully, as it might need to be filled up during the working day. The usual practice was to fill up the tanks from the roadside stream just short of the Dutch House at Sidcup. One night, on the homeward trip, the Farrant vehicle ran low of water in Catford. The driver decided to take a chance and fill up from a horse trough, which was illegal. As luck would have it, a constable appeared and challenged the driver, who responded: 'It's an emergency, constable! If I don't get some water into her she'll blow up.' The policeman vanished so quickly it seemed like magic.

These two chauffeur-driven vehicles belonged to Mrs Harland who lived at Great Bounds. This photograph was probably taken sometime during the First World War.

A Redcar bus on Sceptre Hill. This company began operating bus services in February 1924 in competition with Autocar. It had a fleet of new, small but fast buses and they ran in between the Autocar services and claimed that their intention was to give the public a better service rather than compete head to head with Autocar. The rivalry between the two companies came to a head in January 1928 when a fares war broke out. This became so intense that at one point it was reported that empty deposit-paid bottles were accepted for payment of fares. Further spice was added when Redcar caused Autocar to be fined 5s for operating a bus a third of an inch wider than the legal maximum of 7ft 6in. Both companies found the rivalry financially debilitating and were targets for merger and acquisition. East Surrey gained control of Autocar and Maidstone and District took over Redcar. This stabilised the situation and a working agreement between the two companies was introduced in May 1928.

E. & E. C. Waters were a sister, Emily, and brother, Edward Cecil (always known as 'Sam'), who ran the Waters fruit and vegetable business in Bedford Road. This is Sam with the delivery motorcycle and sidecar in 1936. At the time, Sam was courting Dorothy Tilley and he used to swap the fruit and veg sidecar for a 'Torpedo' sidecar in which she used to sit when they went out on a Sunday. They married in Southborough on 31 May 1936. Emily and Sam took over the business from their mother, Fanny, after Sam returned from doing military service in the RAF during the Second World War.

Most of the fresh food shop businesses in Southborough had their own vehicles and would make daily deliveries to rural areas and villages nearby. Hartridge Brothers were the butchers at 60a London Road from 1904 to at least 1969. It is now Burgess, the butcher.

Nightingale Farm on the Tonbridge side of Bidborough Corner on the London Road had a thriving dairy business before the Second World War. Eggs, cheese, milk and cream were delivered using this motorcycle and sidecar.

Stephen Mercer of 22 Edward Street in 1970 on his 493cc 1930 BSA motorbike (known as a 'sloper' because of its sloping cylinders) which he had bought new for £52. He kept his motorbike in perfect condition as he was a qualified engineer. A bachelor, Stephen took his annual holiday in Torquay, Cornwall, driving there and back every year on his motorbike which did 112 miles to the gallon. He never did own a car. As he told the *Courier*: 'There is no fun in driving cars, especially now when the roads are so crammed.'

G. Hayden was a fruiterer and greengrocer at 6 Pennington Road and the business was run by husband and wife George and Betty in the 1960s. Local deliveries were free and they competed with the bigger supermarkets by giving a personal service and offering a wide range of fresh, mostly locally grown, produce as well as frozen foods, groceries and flowers. They employed various advertising slogans: 'The pick of the crop is in our shop' and 'If their vegetables were any fresher, they would be downright insolent.' The dog sitting in the driver's seat was called 'Lady the Second', or 'Lady' for short, adapted from the Kennel Club pedigree name Lassie Lady of Pennington.

Five
Sport
and
Leisure

Although they were known as the Tunbridge Wells Drum and Fife Band, many of the members were from Southborough. This photograph was taken just before the Second World War. Left to right, back row: Fred Waghorn, Jim Styles, Arthur Parrott (drummer), Eddie Latter (drummer), Mr H.E. Hinton (drum major), Vernon Punyer, -?-, Mr Cedarborg. Front row: Arthur Goddard, George Cane, -?-, Bob Gower (bass drummer), Doug Quinnell (drummer), Len Buckland, unknown person from Rusthall, Fred Jeffrey.

Boys' Brigade
1st Royal Tunbridge Wells Coy. Session 1938-39.

Although known as the 1st Royal Tunbridge Wells Boys' Coy, it was in fact the Southborough contingent of the Boys' Brigade. They used to meet at the Wesleyan chapel, London Road, until it was pulled down in 1936-37. They then moved to the new Methodist church in London Rd. This 1938/39 view shows, left to right, back row: Bob Pring, Ken Young, J. Friend. Third row: Ron Waghorn, Maurice Armand, Ken Bassett, Gordon Bridger, Michael Orford, Harry King, Peter Stone, John Fountain, ? Thorpe. Second row: Norman Page, Norman Cederberg, Jack Fairclough, Captain Cederberg, K. Friend, Sidney Whitlock, George Hook. Front row: Ted Whitlock, John Oage, Len (?) Hallett, Les Sutcliffe, Ted Hartley, John Rickwood, Joe Atkins. Sidney Whitlock was wounded on operations off Cape Gris Nez in the English Channel in 1942, while serving with the Air/Sea Rescue Service of the RAF. He was awarded the Distinguished Service Medal for gallantry following this incident; a rare example of an airman receiving a naval decoration.

Southborough Football Club 1st and 2nd XIs in 1920/21. Arthur Usherwood is second from the right on the back row – the rest are unknown. Left to right, third row: C. Wilson, F.W. Smallcombe, -?-, -?-, -?-, W.J. Bushell, J. Smith, Freddie Littlechild, -?-, -?-, -?-, -?-, E. Jarrott, G. Whitten. Second row: J. Steadman (crouching, in suit), L. Edwards, William Kemp, H. Silver, Ernie Mills (captain), H.R. Brown (club chairman, also chairman of Southborough Urban District Council, the only person to be so honoured twice), Charles Tester, Ernie Denn, Tiny Austen, Harold Hever, N. Langridge (on one knee). Front row: Clarence Tingley, Frank Head, Cecil Cork,-?-. Southborough was very strong at football at this time and in this season won all four major trophies which are on display: Tunbridge Wells League, Tunbridge Wells Charity Cup, Tonbridge League, Tonbridge Hospital Cup. There are also four sets of winners' medals.

The 1922 final of the Tunbridge Wells Charity Shield played at the Prospect Road football ground. Southborough are in the striped shirts and they beat their opponents, Tunbridge Wells.

The Church Army Social Club, High Brooms, 'A' XI, 1924/25. Left to right, back row: George Oxley (linesman and driver for the brick company), Les Gibbs (builder), George Corbett, Bert Hewitt (gasworks employee), Tom Murphy (linesman). Middle row: Harry Gould, Sam Littlechild, Jack Easter, Blackie Brotherhood, Captain Williams (Church Army). Front row: Les Underhill, Albert Battel (one of five brothers who all played football for High Brooms), Harry Hills (plumber), Eddie Hanley, Jack Lambert (worker for Farrant's Haulage and then Baltic Sawmills).

High Brooms Juniors who won the Tunbridge Wells Junior Charity Cup in the 1926/27 season. Left to right, back row: Harry Wilsdon (chairman of the club and a school teacher), Harry Hills, Albert Hewitt, -?-, -?-, either Alf Brown (a local referee) or Mr Crouch (coal merchant). Middle row: ? Jeffery, -?-, -?-, Tubby Cole (?), Charlie Ellis, Mr Scrace. Front row: Brigham Young, Percy Startup, -?-, Harold 'Diffy' Brown.

Southborough Football Club at Meadows School, c. 1948/49. Left to right, front row: Mick Clifton, Fred Waghorn, Tony Walker (Barnardo's boy), Bill Archer, Bob Douglas. Back row: Leslie Reeves (chauffeur at Great Bounds), Gordon Bateman, Vic Huggett, Phil Sale, Jack Willcocks (goalkeeper), Tom Culmer, Doug Dunsford (Barnardo's boy). The Superintendent of Meadows School (Barnardo's) at this time, Christopher G. Hemsley, was very keen to retain good relations between his boys and the town. He encouraged his boys to play for local sports teams and was happy to lend the school's football pitch to the town until Southborough got its own.

High Brooms Toc H Boys' Club football team, 1972. Left to right, front row: Paul Geering, Jon Everest, Malcolm Oakley, Allan Manning, Gordon Smith, Tony Atkins. Back row, left to right: Doug Smith (trainer), Phil Simmons, David Bush, Barry Murrels, Chris Brown, John Murphy, Marjorie Everest (Boys' Club leader).

St Peter's Guides in the 1920s. Left to right, standing: -?-, Ethel Walker, Kathleen Paine, Kathleen Cox, Pat (surname not known), Flo Berry. Seated: -?-, Nellie Cox, Miss Julian (teacher), Miss Jessie Webb (teacher), -?-.

High Brooms Cub Scouts, 1963. Left to right: John Waters, Peter Smart, Jon Everest, Paul Cooper, Martin Pettit, Malcolm Farrington, Anthony Larkin.

St Thomas's Scout Troop's, first ever annual camp to Pevensey Bay, August 1921. Left to right, back row: Arthur Cox (son of Mr W.F.A. Cox, headmaster of St Peter's School), Reverend William Hubert 'Bunny' Andrews (vicar and scoutmaster), Jack Hurst (later chairman of SUDC, 1952-1955). Middle row: Percy Lawrence, Bert Smith, -?-, Frank Shorter, -?-, Tom Twort (later cricket ball maker), -?-, Leonard Sims, Ivan Haggar, Ernest Dear, Norman Martin. Front row:-?-, -?-, -?-, Jack Shorter, Sidney Lowe, Bill Wilson, Keith Styles (?), Douglas Hall, Victor Tanner.

St Thomas's Scout Troop's, annual camp to Albecq, Guernsey, August 1925. Left to right, back row: Frank Shorter, Victor Tanner, ? Playfoot, Bert Lawrence (?), Harold Copper, 'Dad' Faulkner, Douglas Hall. Middle row: Keith Styles, Jack Shorter, Reverend 'Bunny' Andrews (vicar and troop leader), Harry Dent, Ivan Haggar. Front row: Stanley Wirth, Sidney Lowe, Percy Lawrence, Bill Wilson, Bert Smith, -?-.

St Peter's Scout Troop drum, bugle and fife band on the football pitch on the west side of Prospect Road in 1926. The Drum Major and Bandmaster was Mr H.E. Hinton and the bass drummer was Bob Gower.

St Peter's Scout Troop performing a gymnastic display on football pitch to the west of Prospect Road in 1926. The young man in the centre is Bob Gower, the troop band's bass drummer.

St Peter's Scout Troop and Cub Pack in 1926. The adult standing with the flat cap is Mr Etches. Those sitting are, left to right: Mr H.E. Hinton (the bandmaster), -?-, Revd Gardner (curate), Revd J. Russell Howden (vicar), Miss Thorogood (cub leader), -?-. The only other person known is Fred Waghorn who is standing right at the back on the extreme right.

St Peter's Scout Troop summer camp to Felixstowe in 1931. Left to right, back row: George Morley, ? Joy, ? Corke, Bob Gower, ? Morris, ? Funnell, Trevor Reynolds. Middle row: Graham Hyslop, Mrs Hyslop, Revd Sage, Mrs Sage, Jack Hyslop. Front row: ? Corke, Ron Cheesman, ? Divall. Fred Ongley, ? Funnell, Vernon Punyer, Frank Stronghill, ? Funnell.

Southborough Scout Troop in the Parochial Hall in 1967. Back row: Steve Monks, -?-, Trevor Johnstone, Graham Steadman, David Howes, David Bysh. Third row: Peter Jeffrey, Hugh Card, John Howes, Michael Larkin, Robert Romer, ? Crosland, Brian Tilley, Andrew Mear, Chris Lawrence. Second row: Richard Romer, John Earp, David Heritage, Roy Cavie (known as 'Skip'), Bob Constable, Geoff Carrol, Ian Cochrane, John Romer. Front row: Richard Neave, Eddie Webb, Keith Turley, Alan ?, -?-, ? Larkin.

Below opposite: Southborough Cub Scouts in the Parochial Hall in 1967. Left to right, back row: John Puttock, David Knight, Patrick Mitchell, Nigel Hook, Michael Shepherd, Brian Hemsley, Graham Goddard. Third row: Philip Martin, Paul Sands, Roy Talbot, Richard Scholes, Paul Shepherd, Chris Hoff, Stephen Hemsley, Peter Hazelden. Second row: Jeremy Evans, Chris Monks, Mrs Majorie Monks, Mr Sydney G. Romer (leader), Mrs Kit Lawrence, Barry Fitzgerald, Stephen Wright. Front row: Colin Smith, Neil Carpenter, Andrew Ritchie, Robert Campbell (?), Roy Snelling.

Southborough Cycling Club in 1922. Races were sometimes held on the cricket pitch. Bert Langford is on the extreme left; Win Langford is sixth from the left and next to her is Emily Waters.

HAND AND SCEPTRE HOTEL, SOUTHBOROUGH, KENT.

The West Kent Hunt meeting opposite the Hand and Sceptre in 1903.

"THE YEOMEN OF THE GUARD." AT SOUTHBOROUGH. NOV; 1931.

Amateur dramatics have been popular in Southborough over the years, greatly helped by having a theatre in which to perform, largely thanks to the generosity and drive of Sir David Salomons, who had the Royal Victoria Hall built. This is the *Yeomen of the Guard*, performed in November 1931.

Fishing has always been popular for the residents of Southborough and is free in Holden Pond. Today you do not often see girls fishing and you never see cows wandering on the Common any more.

71

I'm
Swanking
at
Southborough

Postcard maker J. Salmon of Sevenoaks produced hundreds of cards for visitors and holidaymakers to send to friends and family back home. This one dates from around 1940 when the tennis club had courts in Prospect Road. To quote the official Southborough guide of this time: 'Visitors say that the air is as exhilarating as that of the seaside, yet tempered by being inland. It is a district essentially suitable to persons suffering from rheumatism ... it is free of dampness and fogs. The sunshine records for the district are remarkably high.' Just before the Second World War, besides the tennis club, Southborough had the cricket club on the Common, two football clubs which used the Yew Tree Road playing field, a rugby football club at Broomhill Park and a hockey club in Park Road. The Wheelers (cycling) Club and the Wattle Badminton Club were also active. The same guide says: 'Southborough is well known among lily growers all over the kingdom for here are the famous nurseries of Mr William A. Constable, the lily specialist', whose business was in Kibbles Lane.

The old roller used by Southborough Cricket Club for over ninety years and sold to Lamberhurst Cricket Club on 20 April 1965. The cricket pitch on the Common was not the only one in Southborough. Robert Winnifrith was the landlord of the Kentish Yeoman in Grove Hill Road, Tunbridge Wells, as well as being a keen cricketer. In 1859 he leased a piece of land from George Newman, a farmer and hop grower of Portland Villa, 139 London Road, Southborough, and laid out a cricket pitch at his own expense. It was located opposite Yew Tree Road, on the corner with Speldhurst Road. In September the same year an All England XI played Tunbridge Wells on this pitch.

Cricket has been played on the Common for more than two hundred years. The Southborough Cricket Club was founded around 1800; the precise date is not known as the records were lost in a fire. There were even matches played by women since a newspaper report recalls that in 1828 the old ladies of Southborough defeated the young ladies of Tonbridge and the winners' prize was three bottles of gin and 3lb of gunpowder tea. For many years boundaries were unknown on the ground and all hits had to be run. In 1898 there was a complaint in the local paper that the crowd watching Southborough was unfair in that they would encroach onto the field when the visitors were batting and so restrict their long hits to ones and twos.

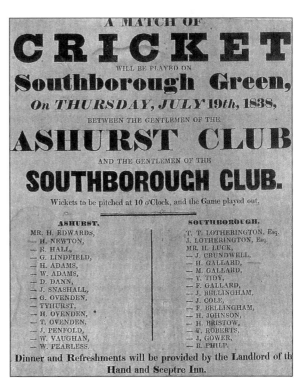

A MATCH OF CRICKET WILL BE PLAYED ON Southborough Green, On THURSDAY, JULY 19th, 1838, BETWEEN THE GENTLEMEN OF THE ASHURST CLUB AND THE GENTLEMEN OF THE SOUTHBOROUGH CLUB.

Wickets to be pitched at 10 o'Clock, and the Game played out,

ASHURST.	SOUTHBOROUGH.
MR. H. EDWARDS,	T. T. LOTHERINGTON, Esq.
— H. NEWTON,	J. LOTHERINGTON, Esq.
— R. HALL,	MR. H. LUCK,
— G. LINDFIELD,	— J. CRUNDWELL,
— H. ADAMS,	— H. GALLARD,
— W. ADAMS,	— M. GALLARD,
— D. DANN,	— T. TIDY,
— J. SNASHALL,	— F. GALLARD,
— G. OVENDEN,	— J. BELLINGHAM,
— TYHURST,	— J. COLE,
— H. OVENDEN,	— F. BELLINGHAM,
— T. OVENDEN,	— H. JOHNSON,
— J. PENFOLD,	— H. BRISTOW,
— W. VAUGHAN,	— T. ROBERTS,
— W. PEARLESS.	— J. GOWER,
	— R. PHILP.

Dinner and Refreshments will be provided by the Landlord of the Hand and Sceptre Inn.

Cricket, Southborough Common. 108.

This photograph was taken sometime before the First World War when soot was used on the wicket to encourage the grass to grow. The umpire in the white coat has got two crutches and only one leg. In 1909 cricket balls (no doubt made locally) cost 3s 9d each and an accident was reported when a young boy fell off his bicycle after riding over one on Sceptre Hill. In 1924 F.E. Woolley, the great England cricketer who lived in Yew Tree Road, agreed to become a vice president of the club. In 1938 Mrs Bertha Godwin began to score for the club and she finally hung up her pencil in 1975.

Below opposite: The 1st XI in 1984. Left to right, back row: C. Young, G. Gilmour, B. Greenwood, K. Bones, P. Young, M. Thomas, J. Pearce (umpire). Front row: P. Hobbs, T. Goodsell, A. Hookway, R. Russell, S. Fisher.

During the Second World War it was decided to suspend matches when an air-raid warning was given. With the help of Lt-Col. Harris, who also turned out for local rivals Bidborough, the club kept going during the war by amalgamating their players to get the occasional game in. In 1955 the new pavilion was officially opened by Lt-Col. Harris and the guest speaker was Colin Cowdrey. When the Duke of Edinburgh visited Southborough in 1964 the club refused permission for his helicopter to land on the cricket pitch and so it had to land on the field at the corner of Pennington Road and London Road. In 1973 the local bylaws were changed to allow the first Sunday game, against Hastings and St Leonard's Priory, on the ground.

The Southborough Cricket Club team around 1898 when Frank Harris was in his prime as a player; he was captain from 1886 to 1935 and a lifelong member of the club until his death in 1957. Left to right, back row: the umpire (name unknown), S. Hammond, F. Gulley, Brooke Hutchings, Bill Draper, W. Muggridge. Seated: Vaughn Hutchings, Tom Godley, Dr Hutchings, Frank Harris, J. Fielder, H. Stapley. Front, on grass: E. Fletcher Jnr, E. King. Dr Hutchings' three sons all played for Kent and the youngest, Kenneth, played for England (see p. 17). In 1903 in the local cricket derby against Bidborough, Southborough were chasing 109 (12 scored by Frank Harris, who also played for the rival village). Southborough only managed to score five in total – they were all out in forty-five minutes with seven players scoring ducks. Apart from one of the openers who scored 2, no runs were scored until No. 9 who scored 2 and No. 10 who was out for 1. W. Carter took the first 5 wickets but was the expensive bowler with 6 wickets for 4 runs off 8 overs with 5 maidens. The other bowler, A. Bird, was the more economical with 4 wickets for 1 run off 7.4 overs. It was during this game that the ostler at the Hand and Sceptre played, but kept having to leave the field to attend to the horses.

Opposite: Albert Mitchell's grave in St Peter's churchyard. As a private (later sergeant) in the 13th Light Dragoons, he was 'one of the bravest of the brave' taking part in the Charge of the Light Brigade at Balaclava in the Crimean War in 1854. He survived the attack on the Russian gun emplacements (forty per cent of his fellow officers and men were killed) and served throughout the campaign, including taking part in the battles of Alma, Inkerman and the siege of Sevastopol. After leaving the army he joined the Kent County Constabulary and lived at 20 Norton Road. He died in 1897 at the age of sixty-seven in his sister's home at 2 Taylor Street.

Six

Military

In

Memory of
ALBERT MITCHELL,
LATE SERGEANT 13TH HUSSARS
AND OF THE KENT COUNTY CONSTABULARY,
DIED 16TH JANUARY 1897,
AGED 67 YEARS.

DECEASED SERVED THROUGHOUT THE CRIMEAN CAMPAIGN
TAKING PART IN THE ENGAGEMENTS AT ALMA,
BALACLAVA, INKERMANN, AND SIEGE OF SEBASTOPOL,
ALSO THE AFFAIRS OF THE
BULGANAK AND MACKENZIES FARM.

THIS STONE WAS ERECTED
BY THE MEMBERS OF THE ABOVE CORPS
AS A TRIBUTE OF RESPECT
TO A BRAVE AND DESERVING COMRADE.

Robert Bertram Pott went out to South Africa in February 1900 as a lieutenant with the first active service contingent of the West Kent Yeomanry, having joined as a trooper some years before. He saw active service in the Boer War and ended up commanding a troop. There was a civic reception for him in Southborough (see p. 43) when he returned to the family home at Bentham Hill House, which was known locally as Pott's Park. This photograph was taken in 1908 when he had been promoted to major and he is dressed in Levee Order.

Captain Pott brought back his two horses, Whisper and Willow Grange, and the regimental mascot dog, Mick, when he returned to Bentham Hill House after the Boer War. On one occasion when the Yeomanry was camped near the Caledon River, Mick began to bark loudly at two o'clock in the morning. Williams, the night stable guard, said, 'I must go round and see what the dog is barking at.' He had gone but a little way when two shots rang out ... then a terrible volley was poured into the sleeping camp and into the horse lines. 'Night attack! Night attack! Turn out!' The writer then says that once the camp was roused, the attack was repulsed, which showed just how much dogs were appreciated by the British soldiers for reasons other than sentimentality.

Mick, with Captain Pott in the pith helmet sitting cross-legged in the front, in South Africa. When the West Kent soldiers were due to return to England, Mick went missing at a transit stop much to the dismay of the soldiers. Captain Pott offered a reward for the truant dog and a few days later Mick was reunited with them just before embarkation. The same writer of the regimental history reported that Mick, in 1902, had been given a comfortable home by Captain Pott and 'was going strong, and wears a beautiful collar studded with Mauser bullets, and with his history on it.' According to family sources, Mick would sometimes wake the house at night, bumping into things and making noises, no doubt dreaming of his adventures chasing the Boers across the veld. Mick is believed to be buried in the grounds of Bentham Hill House but the grave site is unknown and his unique collar awaits discovery at some boot fair or antique shop.

Southborough Detachment of Kent (Fortress) RE (TF) and No. 3 Cadet Company and Band on 30 March 1913, beside the drill hall in Speldhurst Road.

Drivers of 1/3 Field Company RE (TF) at Henley-on-Thames, August 1915. Lt David Salomons is seated in the centre. He drowned along with many of his men when HMS *Hythe* was sunk while approaching the Dardanelles on the night of 28 October the same year. HMS *Sarnia*, a troopship steaming away from the shore after disembarking her troops, collided with the ship carrying the men from Southborough and others. The *Hythe* went down in ten minutes. Captain Salomons refused to leave, standing on the bridge and encouraging his men to keep cool and save themselves. Of the 275 men on board, including the crew, 154 drowned.

Troops of 3 Company, Kent (Fortress) Engineers TF marching through Southborough in 1915. The officer on the horse is Lt David R. Salomons, the only son of the Salomons of Broomhill.

Survivors of HMS *Hythe* at a reunion sometime after the First World War. Mr W.J.W. Pentecost is standing third from the right and Harold J. Grubb is standing on the extreme right. Those seated who have been identified are Mr Tester (first on left), A.F.G. Ruston, who had been company commander at the time (fourth from left), and W.S. Hodges (sixth from left). Second from the left on the back row is Charlie Eliot of 108 Edward Street. After the sinking of the *Hythe*, he was pulled exhausted from the sea. Later in the war, he was sent to the Western Front and had his foot blown off. Gangrene set in and his leg was amputated. After the war he earned his living making cricket balls for Wisden in his garden shed. He supported a wife and five children and his war pension was £1 0s 4d.

Soldiers recovering from their wounds at Holden House in August 1915. The domestic servant on the left is Mrs Edna Stevenson, whose husband Sydney was serving in the Kent Cyclists Battalion patrolling the south coast. He later went to the north-west frontier of India and stayed there for the Afghan War of 1919. He returned to work eventually as the head gardener working for the owner of Holden House, Mrs Morley, believed to be the lady with the cane sitting on the left.

Southborough Home Guard at the Drill Hall in Speldhurst Road, probably in 1941. After the retreat from Dunkirk was completed in June 1940 there was a very real threat of invasion by the Nazis. The Home Guard patrolled mainly at night on the look out for paratroopers and in the daytime put in place road blocks and tank traps (still to be seen beside the green at Modest Corner). In the front row, seventh from the left is Sergeant Major 'Banger' Harris, ninth is Captain Waterhouse (commanding officer) and eleventh, wearing spectacles, is Harry Wilsdon, a well known and popular teacher at High Brooms School. In the second row, ninth from the left is Sergeant Tom Edwards, tenth is Eric Winter and fifteenth is Corporal Jack Lambert.

Warrant officers and sergeants of the Southborough Home Guard, c. 1940. The only person known in the front row is, third from the left, Sergeant Major 'Banger' Harris. In the back row, left to right: Sergeant Eric Winter, -?-, Sergeant Tom Edwards (works manager at the High Brooms Brick and Tile Co.).

Before the Second World War, forty-three milk retailers competed for business in Tunbridge Wells and Southborough. The standard price was 3d for a pint. During the war the Land Army girls delivered the milk on BSA 600cc 'slopers' (the cylinder was inclined). The bikes were serviced by Tim Smart, who was killed at Dunkirk, and Roy Hall, who went on to work for Unigate. The Land Girls' boss was smaller in stature than any of them – Bill Hodges was a survivor of the HMS *Hythe* troopship disaster in 1915 and had been a jockey in the stable of trainer Winston Scott. Hodges did a milk round for forty years and died in 1986. Left to right: Mrs Barker from Hawkenbury; Amy Lewis, a cub mistress in Southborough for many years; Eileen Bray, who narrowly escaped death when her milk bike went under a lorry; Sybil Lye, whose sister Barbara was also a Land Girl; Bessie Miller; and Hazel Dale, who used to work at Marks and Spencer. The women are wearing civilian-style steel helmets put on specially for the photograph taken by *Farmer and Stockbreeder* magazine.

Southborough was in 'Bomb Alley' during the Second World War and enemy aircraft would often drop their bombs at random if they had failed to locate their target, which was usually London. Here Mr Steve Mercer is sweeping garden soil off his shed roof after a bomb had landed in the back gardens of Edward Street. Until 24 July 1944, no V1 (pilotless aircraft) had come down without exploding so the military authorities were keen to examine the one that landed in High Brooms that day. A Land Army girl was feeding chickens and had taken shelter when she heard the engine cut out. As no explosion came, she raised her head cautiously to see 'a dirty great black doodlebug entangled in the chicken wire'. Two RE officers (one being Walter Clary, a current town councillor) were quickly on the scene and evacuated 1,500 nearby residents. They injected the bomb with resin to stop the trigger mechanism working and, whilst the resin was setting they had a cup of tea and a game of cards in a local café. After the doodlebug was rendered harmless there was an argument between the army and the RAF to see who would examine the bomb in detail. The latter won when they pointed out that it had wings. It was towed away on a 'Queen Mary' trailer (used for crashed planes) and it ended up in America. In crashing, the bomb had knocked down an apple tree. The local Air Raid Warden carved some of the wood into a doodlebug and presented it to the bomb disposal squad who were billeted in a garage in High Brooms, as a thank you for their courageous work in defusing the bomb and saving their homes. Southborough shares the distinction, along with Queenborough and Sandwich, of being the only three towns in Kent to have suffered no civilian fatalities from enemy action during the war.

Seven

Work

Miss Ralph, Southborough's first baker's roundswoman, during the First World War. Frederick
Mules & Co. were bakers on the corner of Speldhurst Road and London Road since about 1880.
They were taken over by Paine Smith in 1929.

Hill View Laundry on Victoria Road sometime in the 1920s; its unique selling point was 'open-air drying'. The building was originally a brewery run by a man named Phipps. Using malt and hops only, no sugar, and 'water obtained from the same valleys that supply Southborough with its pure water', it brewed genuine mild, bitter, stock ales and porter and delivered daily to the pubs of Southborough. It ceased to be a brewery in 1895.

Southborough Volunteer Fire Brigade was founded in 1885 and the hose cart was kept at various addresses in the town (for a rent of 1s a week) until the first fire station was built in 1889. The first captain of the brigade was William Loate who had in his charge ten firemen and two messengers whose job was to run round to the men's houses to call them when there was a fire. The volunteer members were paid 1s per hour for attendances at fires. The town's firemen are here marching along London Road in front of the Bat and Ball Inn in around 1910, preceded by the town band. The Local Authority Fire Brigades were merged into the wartime National Fire Service in 1941 and when this was disbanded in 1948 the Fire Service became the responsibility of the Kent County Council. The current fire station opened in 1968. In the twenty years between 1948 and 1968, Southborough firemen turned out to fires and other incidents over 1,300 times. The new fire station cost £11,000. In 1968 the Sub-Officer was H.F. Wallis, with Leading Firemen W.S. Hodge and E.V. Pederson. The firemen were E. Crust, P.A.W. Dunnings, G.J. Farrington, J.E. Foster, F.J. Humphrey, R. Lower, W.L.G. Parker, W. Robinson, B.W. Tompsett, T.J. Wills and G. Worsell.

Opposite: These bakers worked for Southborough company Paine Smith in 1912. They are, left to right: J. Goodwin, W.G. Barnaby, J. Pook, F. Bean and R. Saunders. The Paine family was a well known business family in the town over the years, providing work for many Southborough residents. Their bakehouse in London Road burned down one evening in November 1939 when a gale was blowing. A passenger on the upper deck of a passing bus noticed the fire and jumped off to notify the fire brigade. This was just before 8 p.m. but the premises could not be saved and £3,000 of damage to stock and buildings was sustained. The blackout, because of the Second World War, added to the confusion but it didn't stop a large crowd assembling to watch the blaze.

Public subscription and charity days helped to finance the service and the firemen would give displays, sometimes with their fellow officers from Tunbridge Wells. This photo was taken in 1898 at the charity day for the brigades on the Showfields in Tunbridge Wells. Note the brass helmets and that several men are in fancy dress.

Southborough Fire Brigade was unable to save St Andrew's School when it was burnt down on the night of 8 February 1919. The night was so cold that the water from the pumps froze on the firemen, who had great difficulty with the manual pumps as the pressure was very low. The building was built sometime around 1870 and was taken over in 1891 by Revd Reginald Bull who ran it as a prep school for boys. After the fire the head moved his school to Hammerwood near East Grinstead. The gutted south wing was pulled down and the property sold to Mr Dudeney of Stemps Farm (the Weavers). The old school gymnasium was used as a jam factory for a time and later became Kimber's Garage repair shop and, after that, Caffyns. Many Southborough residents can remember the school swimming pool (near the Yew Tree Road car park) before it was filled in. The North Wing of the house was used as temporary accommodation for council tenants before it was pulled down in 1970.

As a result of the disastrous fire at St Andrew's School in 1919, the town council instructed two members to purchase a motor fire engine. A second hand Renault was purchased (it was thought to be a converted estate shooting wagon) and this was in service in 1927, as seen here. The fire engine had carbide lamps which ran on gas and these had to be lit by hand before leaving the station. The engine was later sold to William Chiesman to irrigate his farm. Leslie Rothwell, himself a Southborough fireman during the Second World War, recognised his father and grandfather in the photograph and has identified several others. They include 'Little' Peter Rothwell, Bill Ralph, Bert Miles, Ernie Mills, Charlie Page, George Rogers, Freddie Kettle, Freddie Littlechild and the Fire Chief, Mr Miles, who lived in Western Road. Until the Second World War the firemen were summoned by a maroon fired from the backyard of the station, which was located next to the Royal Victoria Hall. Maroons were succeeded by a siren which could be heard all over Southborough and this, in turn, was done away with when fire bells were installed in every fireman's house. Now pagers are used.

W. Waters the fruiterer's on the corner of Forge Road and London Road, *c.* 1918. It was incorporated into the Flying Dutchman in 1938. The lady in the doorway is Emily Waters, daughter of William, a farmer from Well Street, East Malling, who took over the business at 110 London Road in 1891 from Thomas Bridgeland. The girl inside the shop is also an Emily Waters, William's grand daughter and she and her brother, Edward Cecil Waters, always known as Sam, eventually had E. & E.C. Waters, the greengrocer's in Bedford Road. Emily died in 1978 and Sam in 1982, when his younger son Roy took over the business. Roy closed the business in 1986 after four generations and almost a century of the Waters family selling fruit and vegetables to the people of Southborough. Roy still lives in Norton Road and the shop bore the name Waters and sold children's items until it closed in September 1998.

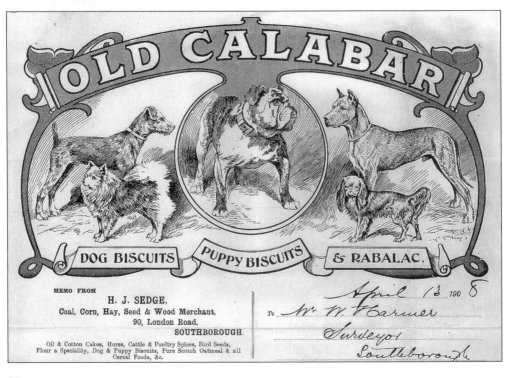

The auxiliary fire-fighters of Southborough during the Second World War at the Old Fire Station in 1941. The diagonal chest bands are the straps that hold their gas masks; note the tapes across the windows to reduce the damage from bomb blasts. As well as dealing with local bombing incidents, they were called to London (Elephant and Castle 11 December 1940, St Paul's 29 December 1940, Southwark Street 16 April 1941, Victoria Street 10 May 1941), Portsmouth in January 1941 and Southampton in November 1941. Left to right, back row: Messenger Ron King, Firemen ? Puttock, Jack Smith, George Wheatly, Bill Sargent, Ern Morley, Percy Vidler, Sam Waters, Harry Moore, Jack Seal, Arthur Raistrick. Front row: Leading Firemen Charlie Wickham, Wesley Hartridge (the only one wearing Wellington boots), ? Burtonshaw, ? Molyneux, Section Leader Harry Bridger, Tom Pearson, Argyle Skinner, Wally West, Len Simmons.

Opposite: Headed note paper of H.J. Sedge whose business was at 90 London Road before and during the First World War. He supplied the inhabitants of the town with coal, corn and hay, as well as all kinds of animal feed including dog biscuits.

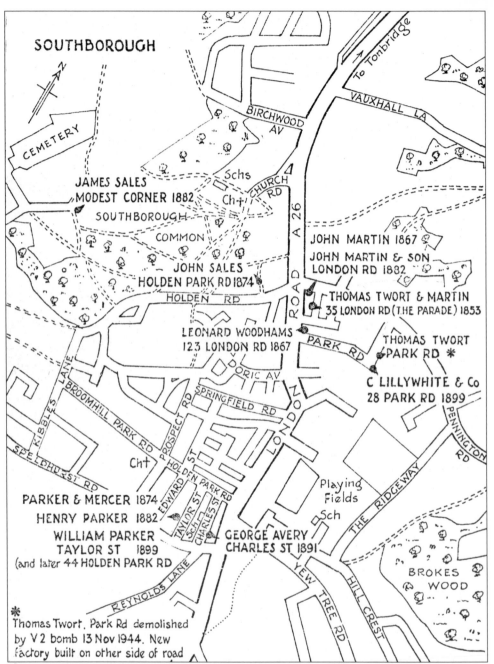

SOUTHBOROUGH

CEMETERY

To Tonbridge

VAUXHALL LA

BIRCHWOOD AV

CHURCH RD

Schs

Ch+

SOUTHBOROUGH
COMMON

JAMES SALES
MODEST CORNER 1882

JOHN SALES
HOLDEN PARK RD 1874

HOLDEN RD

A 26

LONDON ROAD

JOHN MARTIN 1867
JOHN MARTIN & SON
LONDON RD 1882

THOMAS TWORT & MARTIN
35 LONDON RD (THE PARADE) 1853

LEONARD WOODHAMS
123 LONDON RD 1867

DORIC AV

PARK RD

THOMAS TWORT
PARK RD *

C LILLYWHITE & Co
28 PARK RD 1899

PENNINGTON RD

KIBBLES LANE

BROOMHILL PARK RD

SPELDHURST RD

SPRINGFIELD RD

PROSPECT RD

Cht

HOLDEN PARK RD

EDWARD ST

TAYLOR ST

CHARLES ST

Sch

PARKER & MERCER 1874
HENRY PARKER 1882
WILLIAM PARKER
TAYLOR ST 1899
(and later 44 HOLDEN PARK RD

GEORGE AVERY
CHARLES ST 1891

Playing
Fields

Sch

THE RIDGEWAY

BROKES
WOOD

REYNOLDS LANE

YEW TREE RD

HILL CREST

* Thomas Twort. Park Rd demolished
by V 2 bomb 13 Nov 1944. New
factory built on other side of road

The farms of Southborough had two of the necessary raw materials for the cricket ball industry. Cows provided the leather which, of course, was tanned locally as well, and the twine used for growing hops was the original material for sewing the balls together before worsted was found to be better. Thomas Twort founded his cricket ball manufacturing company in 1853 when, in partnership with Mr Martin, he set up in business in London Road with workshops at the rear in Draper Street. Later he moved to Park Street and set up business on his own. In his first year he sold seventy dozen balls for £150 of which £29 was profit. Craftsmen were paid 10s a dozen for stitching the balls.

Founded by Leonard Woodham in 1845, three generations of Woodhams went into the Lion Cricket & Football Works until it was taken over sometime in the 1890s by Dukes, another cricket ball maker. This company is now British Cricket Balls and along with Alfred Reader are the last two British companies to make cricket balls still used in the First Class game – both are Kent-based but no longer in Southborough.

By the time Len Woodham's son had joined his father in business, the Lion brand was on all sorts of sports equipment. This advertisement proclaims that the company is a manufacturer of 'superior cricket balls, bats, leg guards, wicket keeping gauntlets, stumps, tubular India-rubber batting gloves, foot balls, lawn tennis, croquet and badminton' as well as 'complete summer tents and canopies, gymnasiums and all articles connected with British games. Wholesale and for exportation'.

Thomas Twort's sons and grandsons followed him as cricket ball makers. This photo was taken between 1936 and 1939 on a works outing to Windsor Castle. Left to right: Len Woodhams, Bert Bennett, Ted Simpson, Albert Sisely, Alec Brown, George Woodrow, George Chapman, Charlie Tingley, Fred Rosewell, Harry Dent, Amos Eade, Ernest Bachelor, Joe Woodrow, Edwin Twort (the boss). Harry Dent was later mayor of Southborough and a fine player of tennis, badminton and bowls (the Bowls Club has a Harry Dent Cup). Thomas Twort & Sons kept going until it was amalgamated into Tonbridge Sports Industries in 1966. In 1951, during the Lords Test against the South Africans in June, England won and Tattersall had match figures of 12 wickets for 101 runs using a Thomas Twort and Sons cricket ball handmade in Southborough. To celebrate the centenary in 1953, Queen Elizabeth II sent a message of congratulations – one of the workers at that time, Albert Sisely, had been with the business for seventy years and continued to work there until he was eighty-nine.

SOUTHBORO LOCAL BOARD.

To Dustmen, Scavengers, Brickmakers, & others.

PERSONS WILLING TO

CONTRACT

AS

SCAVENGERS,

FOR TWELVE MONTHS,

From the 30th day of November 1872, to the 30th day of November 1873, to remove, and carry away all dirt, dust, ashes, filth, and rubbish, from all houses and premises within the limits of "The Southborough Local Board District," for his or their use or benefit, are to send sealed Tenders to the Clerk, on or before Tuesday, the 26th November, indorsed "Scavenger's Tender."

The Terms of the Contract may be seen at the Clerk's Office.

The Commissioners reserve to themselves the power of rejecting any Tender.

BY ORDER,

GEORGE DELVES, *Clerk.*

1st November, 1872.

In 1872 the Local Board decided at their monthly meeting in October that it should tender for a scavenger. Richard Earl, a brick maker, who lived in Southborough, offered to pay £5 per annum for the privilege of collecting ashes from the district. The tender was accepted on condition that all dust, dirt, ashes, filth and rubbish were collected as well.

Corn was milled at Brokes (sometimes spelt Broakes) Mill for about 100 years until it closed in 1923. The grinding stones were driven by a waterwheel. There were two ponds, now disappeared, which were used to regulate the flow of water to turn the wheel. The last miller was Lewis Manuel who used to deliver the flour to local bakers in a horse and cart with the help in the school holidays of local lad George King who had moved to the nearby cottages from Taylor Street with his family in 1904. Mr Manuel was a keen amateur photographer with box camera, tripod and black cloth and may well have taken this picture. It is dated 1913.

There were two tanyards in Southborough located in the area bounded by the Tanyard Lane, Vale Road and Springfield Road. The first recorded tanner was Richard Waite in 1721. The smell was often quite offensive and the effluent from the tanks – lime, alum, salt and waste material from the raw hides – was discharged into Holden Pond. The larger tanyard tanks were filled in while the site was waiting development after a schoolgirl, Ellen Marchant, aged seven, drowned in one of them on 13 September 1913. The smaller one processed its last leather (stags' hides) in 1922. The man in the photograph is thought to be Mr Christer, who worked for the last owner, George Rye.

A three-storey steam mill was built in 1878 in Western Road (the site of the present day fish and chip shop and Men's Club). It was leased to Mr John Potter and his wife Mrs M.A. Potter. There was a store of army biscuits from the Boer War kept in the top room of the mill and these were sold off after the war as dog biscuits. The mill closed in 1922 and became the Chatfields cycle works and garage. A millstone can still be seen set into the pavement near the fish and chip shop.

During the heyday of the horse and cart there were at least five forges in Southborough. There was E. & M. Starr's coach works and smithy (the site of Birchwood Garage today) which closed in 1910. Vulcan Forge was at the top of Holden Road and closed in 1968 when Tom Reeves, the blacksmith, died. There were forges in Powder Mill Lane and at Holden Corner. The Botten Forge was on Speldhurst Road at the corner of Reynolds Lane. It closed around 1910. This is the forge in Forge Road before the Second World War. Second on the right is William Carter, the blacksmith, and his son, also William, is on the extreme left. It was he who closed the forge in 1946.

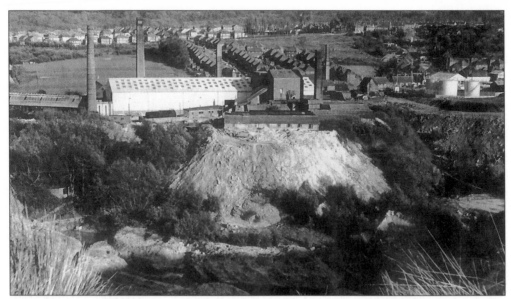

An aerial view of High Brooms Brick and Tile Company works in July 1969, a year after it closed. The view is looking east towards the Sherwood estate. The company supplied bricks for the Dungeness lighthouse, the Blackwall Tunnel, Brighton power station (seven million bricks used) and the Kent and Sussex Hospital in Tunbridge Wells. Rod Chapman bought the brickworks and site. The works were pulled down and the lake drained (it took twelve years and the water board removed the fish to Brighton Lake in Tunbridge Wells). With infilling and levelling the site is now part of the North Farm Industrial Estate.

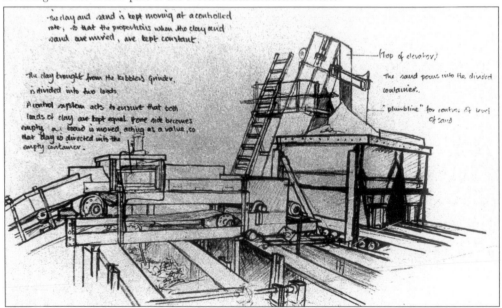

In the summer of 1964 local High Brooms artist Jane Humphrey made a series of twenty-eight sketches of the brickworks, the machines used in quarrying and firing the clay and the workers going about their daily business. Accompanying the sketches are informative notes and they provide a valuable record of High Brooms' most important manufacturing industry. The Southborough Society has copies of the original sketches in its archive.

98

Bricks were made in High Brooms because of the rich seam of Wadhurst clay that occurred locally. The clay was dug out manually, except when it was too hard and explosives were used. Coal was found in the pit in 1895 at a depth of 130ft – it was of good quality and equal to that mined in East Kent but it was of only geological, rather than commercial, interest. In 1933 the bones of an iguanodon were found in the quarry. Casts were made and donated to Tunbridge Wells museum and the originals went to the Natural History Museum in South Kensington.

The quarry workers loaded the trolleys with clay and they were then manually pushed and pulled up to the brick-making sheds. At its peak the brickworks could turn out 100,000 bricks a day but the usual daily output was around 40,000 bricks from each of its two kilns. Workers were paid $3\frac{1}{2}$d for every thousand bricks produced. No money was paid if no bricks were made, so the workers kept going in all weathers.

The clay for the bricks was thrown by hand into moulds in the brick-making shed. When the clay had hardened sufficiently the bricks were turned out of the moulds and were now ready for firing. They were taken to the kilns by wheelbarrows.

After the bricks were fired they were taken by wheel barrow to the yard and stacked ready for sale and distribution. One man estimated that he wheeled $1\frac{1}{2}$ million bricks a year and that during his time with the firm he had wheeled 51 million bricks and walked the equivalent of going round the world twice. This is James Powling, father of Mrs Corbett of Prospect Road, Southborough, in the 1930s.

The brick company had its own steam lorry to deliver the bricks. The worker in the middle is Ted Simmons and on the right is Mr Clifton. Before vehicles were used, the bricks were transported by horse-drawn cart. The stables for the horses were located at what is now the Working Men's Club. In the late nineteenth century, High Brooms Road was just a track and quite steep; it sometimes took the horses laden with bricks three or four attempts to get up the hill (in front of the Working Men's Club).

High Brooms Brick & Tile Co. workers, c. 1960. Sitting on the bench in the front row, fifth from the left (with trilby hat and glasses) is Tom Edwards (works manager), sixth is Teddy Weare (son of the owner), seventh (bald, no cap) is Frank Gerald Craven Weare (owner). Others in the photo are Ben Green, Alec Cavey, Len Vidler, Don Taylor, 'Nobby' Hill (carpenter), and Ernest Johnson. The man standing on the right in the front with the raincoat is Jock Ross, who was a prisoner in Colditz and Douglas Bader's batman during the Second World War. Jock went on to work for R.N. Carr in London Road.

Workers came from as far afield as Staffordshire, Devon and Cornwall, and at its peak the business employed 500, many of whom lived in company houses in High Brooms. These houses were built with local bricks and many are decorated with clay creatures and gargoyles crafted from local clay by the workers and fired in the brick kilns. Many local people resented the

Bentham Farm at the bottom of Victoria Road was a dairy farm which delivered its own milk to the inhabitants of Southborough twice a day. Three generations of the Penticost family ran the farm until the dairy operation was closed in the 1960s. The cart was used to take the fresh milk to the houses in Southborough and the milk was taken from the churns and put into jugs for the housewives to use, once in the early morning and once again after lunch. Later the milk was bottled on the farm. A deep well at Wood Cottage just up from the farm was supposed to be used to keep the butter from melting in hot weather.

workers recruited from outside the area and fights were frequent. The police used always to patrol in pairs. These are the brick yard workers during the Second World War when all the men who could be released for military service were away fighting.

A souvenir postcard of Rosemead, on the corner of Prospect Road and Speldhurst Road. This was a Salvation Army Darby and Joan home for aged couples who would go there for long or short stays. It opened in about 1920 and closed in 1970.

Hops were commonly grown on the farms in and around Southborough. F.J. Podmore was a director of Nightingale Farm along with C.L. Podmore, W.E. Young and J.R. Young. The hops were dried in the oast house and then pressed into pockets which weighed about 1½cwt. 'Poddy' Podmore, as one of the directors was known, was a gruff Lancastrian, former president of Tunbridge Wells Rotary, a keen bowler and secretary of the Tonbridge Branch of the National Farmers' Union. During the First World War he was in the West Kent Yeomanry and taught young troopers to ride. During the Second World War he was Chief Warden in Southborough. He died in 1966 aged eighty.

Hop pickers would come from London to harvest the hops in September and considered the work as their summer holiday in the country. Here pickers are taking the hops off bines which have grown up poles, not strings. Note the horse and cart in the background to take the hops to the oast house for drying. The man with the cloth cap is Harry Duval, the head bin man and the year is 1931.

Eight

Schooldays

Park House was a boys' prep school from about 1890. Mr Freeman was the headmaster. The boys always sat in the front pews of St Thomas' church. In the grounds was a depression which was filled with water in the winter for skating. During the First World War it was requisitioned and became VAD (Kent) No. 98 and Lady Salomons ran it as a convalescence hospital. Later it was a remand home.

St Andrew's Preparatory School (now replaced by St Andrew's Court retirement flats) was built in 1870 and was a school from 1891 to 1919. Here pupils, most wearing school caps and blazers, are working in the gardens.

High Brooms Boys' and Infants' School on Powdermill Lane, 1912. It was founded in 1903. The school motto was 'Play up, play up and play the game' and the cricket and football teams were very successful. In 1920 Charles Malpass was the headmaster and in charge of classes 6 and 7, Mr Livesey took classes 4 and 5, Mr H. Wilson class 3, Miss Baker class 2 and Mrs Malpass class 1. The houses were Gordon (red), Nelson (blue), Wolfe (yellow) and Sydney (green). Mr H.E. Bryson succeeded Mr Malpass as head around 1924.

Staff of St Peter's School, 1913. Left to right, standing: Mr Mercer, Mr Clift, Mr Bocking, Mr Maynard. Sitting: headmaster's son, Miss Capon, Mr W.F.A. Cox (headmaster 1903 to 1929), his daughter and Miss Sharp.

The man in the boater is Mr W.F.A. Cox, the headmaster of St Peter's School on the Common. He was an innovative head whose practice of taking lessons out of doors when the weather was fine was criticized in the national press. Mr Cox came from Bristol where he was coached in cricket, as a boy, by the family doctor, W.G. Grace. The road to Tonbridge was considered unsafe after dark – if the headmaster had a meeting in Tonbridge he would walk to Tunbridge Wells and take the train.

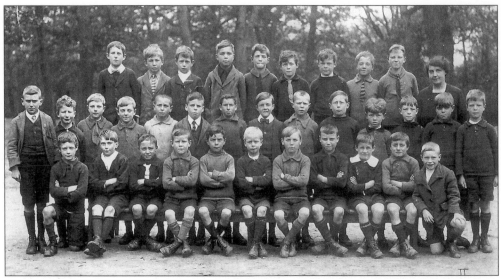

St Peter's Boys' School Class IIB, October 1922. Left to right, front row: Ted Culmer, Harold Dawson, ? Barnaby, Eric Tilley, ? Moon, Peter Lower, Tom Damper, ? Hickmott, ? Shorter, Reg Thorpe, -?-. Middle row: Alf Dadswell, Don Woodrow, Arthur Cox, W. Cox, -?-, W. Shorter, Len Goodwin, Gordon Dear, ? Wickens, Alf Histed, Reg Mercer, ? Taylor, Fred Waghorn, Jack Foster. Back row: Bill Dower, -?-, -?-, Bud Martin, Reg Crouch, ? Crouch, -?-, ? Parritt, -?-, Miss Capon (teacher).

St Peter's girls in 1923; married names when known, are in brackets. Left to right, front row: Nina Lawrence, Adela Damper, Eileen Seal (Winchester), Edith Knight (May), Violet Ellis (Funnell), Elinor Smith, Joyce Standing, Marjorie Smith, Marjorie Burns, Lucy Dadswell. Middle row: Greta Randal, Elsie Ballard, May Wells (Stedman), Vera Mercer (McDougall), Margaret Cannel, Bessie Saunders, Peggy Burns, Ruth Miles, May Stedman, Elsie Jefferies. Back row: Dora Webb, Ivy Joy, Trixie Dent, Hilda Wood, Edith Bryant, Edith Saunders, Winifred Wretham (Jenner), Lily Whitlock.

St Peter's Boys' School *c.* 1929. Left to right, front row: -?-, Tom Culmer, Leslie Baldock, Bill Clarke, John Lawrence, Bernard Williams, Rob Douglas. Second row: ? Morris, Alf Funnell (?), -?-, Leslie Jeffrey, ? Chatfield, -?-, ? Damper, Jack Collins. Back row: Sidney Larter, Frank Begley, other three unknown.

The Holmes Charity School occupied buildings near the present-day Birchwood Garage. In 1775 a trust fund was established by the Rev Edward Holme, sometime vicar of Birling near Maidstone; the trust founded two schools at Leybourne and Malling. One of the trustees of the fund was Revd Charles Wesley, the younger brother of the Methodist evangelist John. Charles is best known for writing more than 5,500 hymns including *Hark! the Herald Angels Sing*. In 1783 Lady Smythe of Great Bounds offered a piece of land in Southborough for a third school and two years later the offer was taken up by the trustees. The school catered for fifty poor boys and girls, thirty-two from the parish of Tonbridge (which included Southborough at that time), twelve from Bidborough and six from Speldhurst. In the early years of the Foundation that looked after the three schools, the visitations of the trustees were more of an outing. They usually spent one night at a local inn carefully chosen for the quality of the dinners provided. Each trustee was allowed to be accompanied by one lady guest, but these guests were later limited to trustees' wives and daughters. One disgruntled assistant master left complaining that he would not stay any longer to hurt his hands boxing the boys' ears. Water for the school was drawn by the pupils from a 70ft deep well and one former pupil remembered that the gardener always wore three hats.

The Holmes Charity School was closed in 1888, but reopened in 1890 as a girls' technical school with Miss Rochester as head. She was succeeded by Miss Maude Lade whose salary was £100 per annum plus the house where she lived with her mother and three of her sisters, one of whom was a pupil at the school. The school closed for good in 1916 and it became a private house called Windy Edge with the annex adjacent called Wesley Cottage.

Charles Street Infants' School, *c*. 1919. Married names, where known, are in brackets. Left to right, front row: Joseph Marchant, Charles Marchant, Charles Whitlock, Harry Whitlock, Jack Kingsbury, Sidney Heaseman, -?-, Daisy West. Middle row: Violet Ellis (Funnel), Jessie Roberts, Ellen Pempathy, ? Pempathy, Ruth Miles (Goddard), ? Miles, Kathleen Saunders, Reginald Mercer. Back row: Gladys West, Queenie Obbard, Maisie Chapman, Margery Culmer, Lily Penfold (Homewood), Bessie Saunders, Hilda Wretham (Scott), Winifred Wretham (Jenner), Vera Mercer (McDougall).

Staff of St Peter's Girls' School in the 1920s. Left to right, front row: Miss Helen Kirby, Miss Emma R. Cox (headmistress from 1894 to 1926), Miss Julian. Sitting on the arms of the seat: (left) Miss Pressnall, (right) Miss Wilson. Back row: Miss Crowhurst, Miss Matthews, Miss Jessie Webb.

St Peter's Girls' School Standard VI (second highest class) in 1928. Left to right, front row: -?-, Marjorie Penticost, Lily Steadman, Beatrice Green. Second row: Helen Clarke, Lorna Haggar, Gladys Long, -?-. Third row: Nina Lawrence, Grace Standing, ? Wenham, Irene Smith. Back row: May Wells, Edith Jeffreys, Phyllis Humphreys (standing), -?-, Kath Saunders.

St Peter's School, Mr Pearson's class, 1959/60. Left to right, front row (married names, where known, in brackets): Brian Thomas, Peter Gibbs, Christopher Gillmore, Stephen Taylor, Roy Matthew, Robert Baldock, Graham Stedman. Second row: Fay Kenyon, Linda Roswell (Higgins), Carol Stedman, Linda Collier, Carol Tipping, Janet Foreman (Vigar), Susan Tapp, Ria Buckwell, Jennifer Woodhams (Barclay). Third row: Susan Barrett, Carol Sutton, JoAnne Wheeler, Jennifer Collier, Andrea Pring (Farmer), Gillian Pope, Margaret Seal, Susan Lemon, Christine Bryant (Waterman). Back row: Barry Wickens, David Collier, Peter Willmore, Anton Wittwer, Andrew Weir, Richard Cripps, Roger Cane, Richard Vidler.

Nine

Outlying Districts

Bentham Hill House bedecked with bunting to welcome home the owner, Captain Pott, from the Boer War. The house was completed in 1832 using local sandstone and bricks to a design by Decimus Burton. In the stable block is a memorial to Greybeard, a horse that gave loyal service to the family for twenty-two years. Its grave, and that of another horse called Bogie, is nearby. The house eventually came under the ownership of Reliance Insurance who sold it off as private flats.

Modest Corner on the west side of the Common is a very old settlement with at least two timber-framed houses – Wood Cottage and Cheynes Court (No. 22) – probably built in the sixteenth century. A number of the home owners still have Commoners' rights of estovers (wood for repair and fuel), turbary (digging turf), piscary (right of fishing) and pannage (right to allow pigs to eat acorns and beech mast). The delivery cart in the photo is that of George Paine, the Southborough baker. Commoners and local farmers had the right to graze animals on the Common and this was exercised as can be seen by the close-cropped grass. As recently as 1968 owners claimed these rights although nobody now takes them up – for example, the owner of 22 Modest Corner has the right to graze two oxen, two pigs, two sheep, two goats, four geese, twelve fowls, one horse and one donkey 'together with the followers of any of the said animals' on the Common.

Good clean drinking water was an imperative once the town began to expand in the latter half of the nineteenth century. In 1884 the town thought the problem of a clean scource of water was solved when Mr Pott of Bentham House allowed water to be taken from the springs in the wood on his estate and to be pumped by a purpose built engine house at the foot of Bentham Hill to a reservoir holding 100,000 gallons behind the Holme School at the top of Sceptre Hill. The flow of the spring varied between 1,000 and 9,000 gallons an hour. But demand for drinking water kept increasing and so it was decided to drill an artesian well (as in the photograph) next to the pumping station to secure more water. This was done in 1897, but despite going down 450 feet, there was insufficient water and the well was abandoned. A second supply of water was eventually obtained from a well sunk at Hayesden.

The Hilly Fields off Pennington Road, seen here in 1910, have always provided fine views. In 1986 the land was acquired by Southborough Council and became a detached part of the Common. Pennington Road takes its name from Robert Rainy Pennington, of Portman Square in London, who owned land here which he left to his nephew George James Pennington in 1841. Vauxhall Lane used to come through Honnington Farm to Pennington Road at the top of the Hilly Fields (the footpath follows the old track) – it was an important access to the iron workings in the valley. Slag from the furnaces and forges was used as road material to reduce the damage done by the heavily-laden carts.

Mabledon lost its two lodges and thirty acres mainly of woodland when the slip road and main Tonbridge by-pass were built in 1969. The lodge in the picture was built of the same stone as the house. It was quarried on site and hardened with exposure, so becoming very durable. The original big house was built by James Burton in 1804 and it was he who bore much of the expense in re-routing the Quarry Hill road past the lodge house and away from the main house, cutting away the hill to ease the gradient. This was done between 1806 and 1808 and this former turnpike road became the first stretch of macadamized road in Kent. Prior to this date Quarry Hill was often virtually impassable in bad weather as horses struggled to pull carts and coaches up the steep hill.

Mabledon as it is today is very different from the house that was built on the same site in 1804 by the London architect and builder James Burton. James's more famous son, Decimus (born in 1800 and so named because he was the tenth child of twelve, six boys and six girls), spent his childhood here before the house and estate was sold to John Deacon of the banking family in 1830. John Deacon II (eldest son of the original purchaser) changed the modest country home into the veritable mansion seen today, including the tower. This is Mabledon before the house was transformed by Decimus Burton, the architect who drew up the new plans for his erstwhile home for the Deacon family.

The Deacon family of Mabledon was very religious and the tower bears the Biblical inscription from Proverbs 18:10: 'The Name of the Lord is a strong tower, the righteous runneth into it and is safe'. With the death of John Deacon II in 1901, the estate passed to his son, also John, and he lived there with his two sisters Jane and Beatrice; none of the three siblings ever married. They lived nonetheless in considerable comfort with forty-five servants, including ten maids, ten gardeners, four game keepers and two footmen. During the Second World War it was requisitioned for military purposes and there were fifty Nissen huts on the site (Mr Deacon was allowed to retain a flat over the library). Field Marshal Montgomery officially opened the place as an officers' training depot. After the war the Ministry of Health took over the building as a psychiatric hospital for Polish soldiers and refugees with Dr Bram, of Swiss-Polish extraction, in charge. Following that it reverted to what the last member of the Deacon family had wished – a home of rest for retired clergy and as a Christian conference centre with strict no-smoking and no-alcohol rules throughout the house. The Trustees of J.F.W. Deacon, who died in 1941 and whose two sisters predeceased him, sold the property to a private buyer in 1992.

Holden Pond has always been a popular place for feeding the ducks and fishing. Pollution was sometime a problem as the pond was downstream from the tannery just off Holden Road and it was only in 1861 that the main drain across Southborough Common was diverted into a filter instead of directly into the pond. In 1864 Mr Crundwell, who owned the Tanyard, was ordered not to use the ditch that discharged into Holden Pond to dump his refuse, lime and filth. Cesspits and sewers in Holden Road had always been a problem as they were in close proximity to wells used for drinking water. In cold weather the problem was exacerbated because the cesspools would freeze over. In December 1871 the Local Board requested tenders to empty the pools; 'one gentleman was willing to empty them for £9 on condition that he could have the contents.' Local councillor Walter Clary has been a self-appointed warden of Holden Pond for many years. In 1995 he fished out of the pond a three foot crocodile (stuffed) that he took home and placed beside his own garden pond as a cat scarer.

Little Boundes was built in 1689 to serve as the Dower House to Great Bounds owned by the Smythe family of Bidborough. The timber frame for the house was cut and shaped in Penshurst and the pieces transported to Southborough where it was assembled. Catherine of Braganza, wife of Charles II, stayed there once. The great preacher John Wesley stayed and preached there on four occasions in 1762, 1764, 1769 and 1774. He was a guest of the owner Sir Thomas I'Anson and his family and on each occasion the house was filled to overflowing. As a boy Samuel Wilberforce, third son of the slave trade abolitionist William, lived with the Revd J. Spragge, the curate at Bidborough, at Little Boundes and was taught by him. He left his mark in Southborough by scratching his initials on a bathroom window in Little Boundes. Samuel went on to become the Bishop of Winchester and was killed when he fell off his horse in 1873.

Great Bounds is an ancient estate originally part of the land belonging to Tonbridge Castle. It takes its name from John Bounds who acquired it in the fourteenth century. The manor was confiscated by the Crown when Edward Stafford, the Lord of the Manor, was found guilty of treason and subsequently Henry VIII granted it to Sir Thomas More, English statesman and scholar, in 1532. He is most famous for displaying 'primitive virtue and simplicity' in high office and his refusal to consider nobody else but the Pope as the head of the church cost him his life – he was tried for treason and beheaded in 1535. During his time at Great Bounds, More was visited by Erasmus, the Dutch humanist and scholar, who preached in Bidborough church. During the Second World War the house and grounds were commandeered by the Army and Canadian troops were stationed there prior to D-Day. By 1958, the fabric of the building was so bad that it had to be pulled down.

The Bounds Oak in the eponymous Bounds Oak Way was reputed by *Strutt's Forestry* (a survey of the woodland of England) to be 1,000 years old. However, contrary to popular opinion, the tree is *not* mentioned in the Domesday Book. The tree was 26ft in circumference (measured at a height of 5ft from the ground). The site of this ancient tree can still be seen today - a replacement oak has been planted near the Tonbridge end of the road on the east side. The hollow trunk of the old tree was still a landmark in the 1960s.

Ivy House Farm in Pennington Road is probably the oldest house in Southborough, built around 1460. It was formerly called Kipping Hall, deriving this name from the family of iron masters who lived in the area when the house was built. The Streatfeild family of Chiddingstone owned it for many years in the seventeenth century and later the Twort family, tanners and cricket ball manufacturers, owned it in the eighteenth century. This picture from 1880 shows the timber frame covered up with weather boarding. The tenant farmer was Edward Wickens at that time and his main crops were arable and hops. Fred Stevens acquired the farm in 1893. By 1923 F. Webster was living there and he gave his occupation as dairyman.

Broakes (Brokes) Mill, Powdermill Lane, has been an industrial site since at least 1552 when the Lord of the Manor of South Frith, the Duke of Northumberland, hired an iron founder, Robert True, to operate a forge and furnace here. They were on separate sites on the same stream and the hammer for the iron foundry was worked by a waterwheel as was the bellows for the furnace. The next industrial use was the manufacture of gunpowder. Place names in the area – Cinderfield, Forge Wood, Forge Farm and Minepit Wood – give clues to what went on here. Local alder wood was made into charcoal and this was used in the manufacturing process. Saltpetre was also needed and this was obtained from droppings in dovecotes, cow byres or human cesspits. The gunpowder mill closed sometime in the early nineteenth century and by 1845 there was a small corn mill on the site and the miller's name was Henry Peerless. The mill continued to make flour until it stopped operations in 1923. The last miller was Lewis Manuel.

Southborough Common is well known for its mature oak and beech trees. There was a quoits pitch in the seventeenth century, probably on the site of the cricket pitch. This view is of the cross roads between Constitutional Hill and Victoria Road around 1910. A horse-breaking ring was located on the St Peter's side of the Common on the corner between the bridle path that leads to Modest Corner and Victoria Road. Frank Street was the horse breaker in 1878. A temperature of 106°F was recorded on Southborough Common in 1906. Residents whose properties border the Common still pay a guinea (£1.05) annually for the right to cross the Common to their property. The old gravel pit on the Common used to have a pond in it. When Holden Pond was last cleared out the mud was trucked to the pit and dumped.

In the *Southborough Official Guide* (Ninth Edition) published in 1941 the Common is described: 'Flaring holly trees, grey-green juniper bushes and stretches of heather and bracken add variety of colouring in any weather, and to stand amid the golden glory of the gorse is enough to cheer the most dismal of mortals.' This is looking up Holden Road to the South of France.

Ten

Salomons and Broomhill

The two Memento Rooms are where the Salomons family treasures, souvenirs and memorabilia are displayed for the public to view. Three generations are recorded – the first baron was Sir David Salomons (1797-1873) who married Jeannette but they had no children and the baronetcy passed to Sir David's nephew, Sir David Lionel Salomons. He married and had five children, four daughters and a son and heir, David Reginald, who died before he could inherit when HMS *Hythe* was sunk during the Gallipoli campaign in 1915.

The first Sir David Salomons Bt (1797-1873) bought Broomhill, a 'very elegant small villa' set in extensive grounds, at Christie's auction in 1829. Presumably he knew the area well because he had been brought up on his father's (Levy Salomons, 1774-1843) estate in Frant. Sir David soon set about converting his new property into a substantial country house with the assistance of Decimus Burton who was familiar with the area, spending his formative years at Mabledon when his family moved there in 1804. The Salomons did not move to Broomhill till 1852. Sir David made his money in finance; he was a member of Lloyds and the Stock Exchange and was a founder member and director of the London Westminster Bank. He was also much engaged in public duty. He was elected as a liveryman to the Worshipful Company of Coopers in 1831 and he became Sheriff of London in 1835. In 1839 he was Sheriff of the County of Kent. By 1847 he had become Master of the Coopers and so an alderman of the City and in 1855 he became the first Jewish Lord Mayor of London. He was most proud, as Lord Mayor, of persuading the Common Council to remove from the Monument to the Great Fire the words attributing the fire to 'malice and hatred of Roman Catholics.' As an MP he continued to fight for political rights for minorities – not just Jews, but Roman Catholics and Quakers as well.

Sir David Lionel Salomons inherited his baronetcy (by special remainder) and Broomhill from his uncle Sir David when he died in 1873. The second baron's interests were both intellectual and practical – he was an inventor, an engineer, an electrician and a craftsman in wood, ivory and metal. In 1874, for example, he was granted a patent for his invention of an automatic railway signalling system. Even though his uncle had carried out a lot of improvement work on the estate, Sir David set about designing (with the exception of the stables) and building further extensions and additions to Broomhill right up to the outbreak of war in 1914.

The stable staff during the 1880s. Mr Walter Nunn, the head coachman, is sitting in the centre; he was retrained as a chauffeur when horseless carriages replaced the horses and carriages. When Sir David Lionel inherited Broomhill in 1873, the stable and coaching staff were important to the owner for discharging his civic and business duties. Even though labour was comparatively cheap for such a wealthy man, Sir David Lionel soon set about designing and building labour-saving devices which were way ahead of their time. In the stable block, he had automatic mechanical watering and feeding systems for the horses and he built a complete veterinary hospital adjacent to it and a forge for the blacksmith to shoe the animals. The stable block had accommodation for twenty-one horses and twelve carriages and was built between 1890 and 1892 in a distinctive French chateau style. It cost £27,000 then, which is about £1 million in today's money.

The west side of Broomhill in the late nineteenth century. The water tower had been built in 1876 and an observatory incorporated into the spire at the top. Sir David Lionel had this removed when his interest in astronomy was eclipsed by those in motor cars and engineering, especially as his health began to suffer because he was spending so much time in the cold night air. The worker in the foreground is using a double-handed scythe to cut the grass for hay.

Broomhill was the first private house in the country to use electricity for cooking and other domestic work, including an iron and a sewing machine. As early as 1874 an arc light had been rigged up in Sir David Lionel's workshops and by 1882 there were sixty lamps of fifty volts. By 1896 a dynamo had been installed for 1,000 sixteen-candlepower lights. The house supplied its own electricity until it was connected to the Tunbridge Wells electricity generator in 1911.

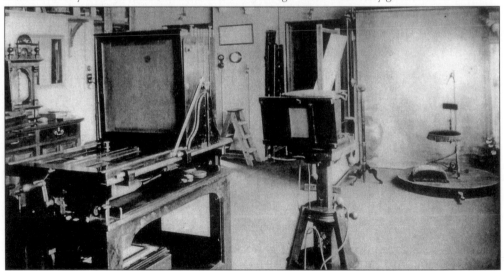

The photographic studio was built by Sir David Lionel onto the back of his theatre along with dark rooms and a chemical laboratory. He was a very keen photographer and invented an electric exposing camera in 1870. In the theatre, he experimented with and showed cinematograph films and installed an ingenious mechanism for mechanically drawing the shutters over all the windows to effect complete darkness. He was elected a Fellow of the Royal Photographic Society in 1895.

Sir David Lionel Salomons and his 1898 Peugeot. Sir David was an expert on motor mechanics before most people had ever heard of the internal combustion engine. He organised the first motor show in England at Tunbridge Wells in 1895 on the agricultural showground off the Eridge Road (now Showfields estate). There were five vehicles on display - the total number of cars in the UK at that time. These were his own Peugeot, Evelyn Ellis' Panhard-Levassor, one motor cycle, one fire engine and one steam engine towing a carriage. It was not illegal for cars to be driven on the public highway but it was illegal for them to exceed 2mph, as they were discriminated against by the Locomotives Act of 1865. The same restrictions did not apply to horse transport, or even to cyclists, so motorists were harassed not for driving, but for speeding. Because of these restrictions he got up early and drove the vehicles from Broomhill to the showfield. He returned to Broomhill to take his family and guests in a horse carriage to see the vehicles. When he arrived back on site he unhitched the horses and posted a notice HORSELESS CARRIAGE which was his idea of a joke! As his interest in motor cars grew, Sir David rebuilt his old stables and they remain what is probably the finest example of early motor-carriage houses anywhere in Britain thanks to his customary expertise and eye for detail. These five garages (still with their original doors and hinges) had cavity walls, central heating, tongued and grooved boarded ceilings, inspection pits (at just the right depth for the chauffeur/mechanics to stand in) and a spiral staircase leading down from the chauffeur's quarters. Alfred C. Harmsworth wrote *Motors and Motor Driving* in 1902 (published by Longmans Green) and Sir David contributed the chapter on *The Motor Stable and its Management*. The Honourable C.S. Rolls (half of the famous Rolls-Royce marque) was a frequent visitor to Broomhill.

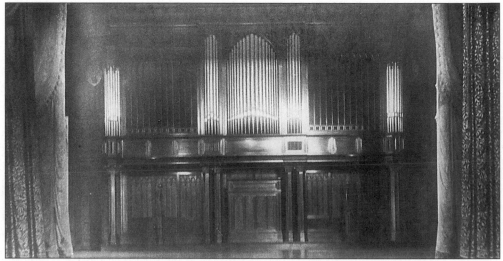

The Welte organ is probably unique as it was built to individual specifications for Sir David (the Allies bombed the Welte factory during the Second World War and the Salomons' organ plans were destroyed). It cost £4,050 in 1914 and arrived just one week before war was declared. At Broomhill are over 250 organ rolls made by great organists of the past including Gigout, Lemare, Hollins, and Goss Custard. Although it can be played manually Sir David Lionel, who described himself as 'a born mechanic', preferred the mechanical performance. The organ has not been played since Sir David Lionel's death and the Sir David Salomons Society is dedicated to raising a considerable sum of money to have it restored to its former glory but this is well under way with an award of a National Lottery grant.

Captain David Reginald Salomons in the uniform of the Royal Engineers in 1913. The only son of Sir David Lionel and his wife, David Reginald went down with HMS *Hythe*. Educated at Eton and Gonville and Caius, Cambridge, Captain Salomons raised a detachment of Territorials in Southborough which was mobilized in 1914 after the outbreak of war – these men became part of the 1/3 Kent Field Company, Royal Engineers. With the sinking of the *Hythe*, 128 men of the company and one officer were drowned. Their memorial is in St Matthew's church, High Brooms.

With the death of Sir David Lionel in 1925, the male line of the family came to an end, as his son had drowned in 1915. His widow, Lady Laura Julia, died ten years later and Broomhill passed to their daughter Mrs Vera Bryce Salomons (1888-1969). In 1937 she gave Broomhill to Kent County Council and it was renamed David Salomons House. She expressed the wish that it be used 'for the benefit of the people of Kent' with covenants limiting it to be used as a technical institute, college, museum, memorial hall, institute for scientific research or public park or as a convalescent home or hospital. During the Second World War it was used as a hospital for wounded soldiers and airmen as seen here in 1942. The lady in the centre in the bonnet was Miss P.I. Pisani. Of the three men in suits standing on the left, third from the left is Ernest Cosham, the head gardener. In 1948 Broomhill became the property of the Ministry of Health following the creation of the National Health Service. It's now called Salomons Centre and is a conference and training facility.

This photo was taken by Sir David Lionel in 1870 using his electric exposing camera that he had invented. It shows the staff of Broomhill. His photographic work led him to experiment with X-rays and he presented several hospitals with the necessary equipment and used to install it himself. At the New Year Sir David Lionel used to send his friends small booklets of maxims he had composed during the year. These included: 'Never pat a strange dog with no tail to wag' and 'Collecting is a form of madness, but a graceful insanity when applied to works of art'.